The Forgotten Luther III

*To Ann
with much love,
Paul*

The Forgotten Luther III

Reclaiming a Vision of Global Community

CONRAD A. BRAATEN AND RYAN P. CUMMING, EDITORS

FORTRESS PRESS
MINNEAPOLIS

THE FORGOTTEN LUTHER III
Reclaiming a Vision of Global Community

Cover image: © iStock 2021; Flat planet Earth icon stock illustration by Daria
Kashurina
Cover design: Alisha Lofgren

Print ISBN: 978-1-5064-6691-0
eBook ISBN: 978-1-5064-6692-7

This study book and the symposium that produced it are dedicated to the glory of God and with thanksgiving for those who have given visionary and creative leadership to the global mission of the church through the Evangelical Lutheran Church in America and its predecessors.

Bo Sorenson—American Lutheran Church

David Vickner—Lutheran Church in America

Jim Mayer—Association of Evangelical Lutheran Churches

Mark Thomsen—Evangelical Lutheran Church in America

Bonnie Jensen—Evangelical Lutheran Church in America

Rafael Malpica Padilla—Evangelical Lutheran Church in America

Contents

Acknowledgments

The planners of the Forgotten Luther project would like to express a profound word of gratitude to our hosts for the symposium *The Forgotten Luther III: Reclaiming a Vision of Global Community* in October 2019: Rev. Connie A. Miller, senior pastor of Saint Luke Lutheran Church (Silver Spring, Maryland); Deacon Kyle Warfield; and the Forgotten Luther local planning team at Saint Luke Lutheran Church. The symposium partnered with Saint Luke's lecture series, benefitting immensely from their team's meticulous planning, generous financial support, videotaping, livestreaming, publicity, registration, catering, and overall hospitality. It has been so important in the Forgotten Luther project that the symposia out of which our congregational study books have emerged were based in congregational ministry. In this context, we would again like to express our gratitude for the hospitality that we enjoyed during the first two Forgotten Luther symposiums at Church of the Reformation in Washington, DC, and to Rev. Michael Wilker, senior pastor. The Forgotten Luther working group at Reformation did a magnificent job. We have been encouraged, not only by the generous congregation-based effort and support from both Reformation and Saint Luke, but by their commitment to the underlying thesis of the Forgotten Luther. We give thanks, with the hope and prayer that their efforts will provide the opportunity for many more congregations to wrestle with the implications of the forgotten Luther in our time.

Abbreviations

LQ   *Lutheran Quarterly* (1987–)

LW   Jaroslav Pelikan and Helmut Lehmann, eds., *Luther's Works: American Edition*, vols. 1–55 (St. Louis and Minneapolis: Concordia and Fortress, 1955–86); vols. 56–82, ed. Christopher B. Brown and Benjamin Mayes (St. Louis, MO: Concordia, 2009–)

WA   Martin Luther, *D. Martin Luthers Werke (Weimarer Ausgabe)*, 136 vols. (Weimar, Germany: Hermann Böhlau, 1883–2009)

Introduction

"A New Heaven and a New Earth"

PAUL WEE AND CONRAD A. BRAATEN

THE GLOBAL VISION

The crisis in which the global community finds itself today—with the coronavirus pandemic, economic and political uncertainties, environmental threats, and a pervasive anxiety about the stability of social institutions—provides an occasion to ask some serious questions about the future shape of our life together. As we are all quite aware, these questions are not simply theoretical but affect our daily existence. They clearly preoccupy those who are engaged in the project, *The Forgotten Luther III: Reclaiming a Vision of Global Community*. Along with congregational members who share the same fears and hopes, those who have contributed to this study book have brought not only imagination and scholarship to the task but an overwhelming sense of urgency as well.

Amid a sea of changes during his time, Heraclitus is said to have lamented, "Everything flows. Give me a place where I can stand."[1] For the church, that place is God's eternal word. This is our first point of reference, a "given" for the Christian community. It is from the vantage point of the event of Jesus Christ that we view the expanse of history. As the expression "A new heaven and a new earth" (Rev 21:1) suggests, any project that seeks to give shape to a new global vision will find its inspiration here, in Holy Scripture, in the revelation of the meaning and direction of history.

A key element in Saint John's apocalyptic vision is God's ultimate triumph over the forces of darkness. That is our vision as well. Set in the midst of the turbulent days of the late first century, the drama depicted by Saint John in his circular letter is cast in an array of colorful images whose

---

1. H. Stuart Hughes, *Consciousness and Society* (New York: Routledge, 2017), 230.

meaning is not readily apparent to everyone. To the forces of oppression, it is simply a collage of meaningless legends. But to the community of the Way, rooted as it is in the stories of liberation, the images hold a powerful message of transformation and hope. For then and for now, the message revolves around the one who brings the new creation, who proclaims, "See, I am making all things new" (Rev 21:5).

This study book for congregations is intended, in the spirit of Saint John, to call the church to a new sense of what a world refashioned in light of God's word might look like. Inspired by the letter of Revelation, written to help the seven churches of Asia Minor respond to the oppressive demons of the first century, this study book seeks to address God's word to the community that faces the demons of the twenty-first century. Just as Saint John speaks of judgment as well as renewal, the contributors to this study are likely to say things that will initially shock but will ultimately invigorate. So—in that spirit—take a deep breath, brace yourself, and open your mind to participate in an exercise of preparation for what is to come. It is our hope that this modest book will find Christian people who are eager to be better equipped to meet, with creativity and confident faith, the major crises of our day.

THE PRESENT CONTEXT

It is no secret that our present crisis has something to do with the global governance, with the special role of governing authorities. As the deadly COVID-19 pandemic began to sweep across the world, the Evangelical Lutheran Church in America's (ELCA's) presiding bishop Elizabeth Eaton addressed the issue in a public statement. It began as follows: "In 1527 the [bubonic] plague returned to Wittenberg, Germany. Two hundred years earlier the plague had swept across Europe killing up to 40% of the population. Understandably, people were anxious and wondered what a safe and faithful response might be. In answer to this, Martin Luther wrote 'Whether One May Flee From a Deadly Plague.' In it, he emphasized the duty to care for the neighbor, the responsibility of government to protect and provide services to its citizens, a caution about recklessness, and the importance of science, medicine and common sense."[2] If one were to give a capsule statement of the goal of our multiyear effort to bring to light what we have called "the Forgotten Luther," it might best be summarized in Bishop Eaton's reference to Luther's biblically grounded claim that it is the God-given "responsibility of government to protect and provide

---

2. Evangelical Lutheran Church in America, "ELCA Presiding Bishop Addresses Concerns about COVID-19," ELCA.org, March 6, 2020, https://www.elca.org/News-and-Events/8025.

services to its citizens." Such an affirmation has nothing to do with partisan politics; it has everything to do with the role of the state under God.

For the faith community rooted in the biblical tradition, "government" is neither autonomous, as if the state were a law unto itself, nor a "divine right," as if rulers were those upon whom a special privilege had been bestowed. Rather, it means that all government, in its many variations, is responsible in its actions to the one Creator God of justice and peace, to the one of whom it is written, "All the nations belong to you!" (Ps 82:8).

This assertion about the role of government—grounded as it is in the prophets, in Jesus Christ, in the letter of Revelation, and in the confessional tradition of the Reformation—belongs neither to the academy nor to the church alone. It belongs to the people. As recent history has demonstrated with such deadly clarity, the question about the proper role of government is well beyond the borders of partisan debate. For those within the church and those without, whatever your political persuasion, how it is answered can make the difference between sickness and health, between death and life. It is abundantly clear going forward that the lives of millions, in North America and throughout the global community, will depend on how it is answered.

THE MESSAGE FROM THE GLOBAL SOUTH

If you have followed the thesis of *Forgotten Luther* in volumes 1 and 2, you will know that a major impetus behind this call to think differently about the gospel and how Martin Luther was grasped by its power comes from theologians of the church in the Global South. As Tim Huffman, retired professor of Christian mission at Trinity Lutheran Seminary, wrote so passionately in *Forgotten Luther* volume 1, it is they who have reminded the whole church that the gospel makes an "ineluctable move from justification to justice." It is they who have not only written about this move but embodied it in their own lives, sometimes at great personal sacrifice. So be prepared, as Huffman states, to face "a challenge to the way things are—to systems that perpetuate class divisions and justify income inequality." Asking whether "Lutheranism can be re-energized by that revolutionary character of our own theological heritage 500 years later," he answers in the affirmative. Acknowledging that "a crisis is a terrible thing to waste," he calls on the church to face it with creativity and hope.[3]

This third volume seeks to explore the roots of ministry in the Reformation tradition, with special emphasis on the link that Luther made between justification and justice. This is expressed in his interaction with

3. Carter Lindberg and Paul Wee, eds., *The Forgotten Luther: Reclaiming the Social-Economic Dimension of the Reformation* (Minneapolis: Lutheran University Press, 2016), 69, 72, 75, 76.

political leaders in his work to bring about a more equitable distribution of wealth, eradicate poverty, and establish health care for all and state-sponsored education for girls as well as boys. With particular reference to contributions from churches in the Global South, this study book hopes to inspire, equip, and embolden congregations in the North to follow a similar path. It is the challenge of "global mission" today. Many of course are already there.

THE NEW SHAPE OF GLOBAL MISSION

Based on the manner in which Luther not only preached God's free and unmerited grace but also drew its concrete implications for the daily lives of the people, he would, we suggest, wholeheartedly welcome the shift that has taken place in the understanding of the global mission of the church. This shift has come about not only as churches in the Global South have become more self-reliant but also as they have sought to respond creatively to immense social, economic, and political challenges. They have developed indigenous spiritual, human, and material resources for the task and have in the process forged new bonds of cooperation with churches in the North.

This partnership centers on mutuality. Already in the late 1960s, the Lutheran World Federation (LWF) produced a documentary entitled *Mission on Six Continents*. In many ways, this documentary heralded a significant transition in global mission perception. This perception had been gradually emerging as churches in the Global South, many the product of classical "missionary" endeavors by European and North American church bodies, were bold enough to say to colleagues in the North, "You are not only part of the solution to our suffering; you—and the economic and political systems you represent—are part of the problem."

Rather than being offended by such a claim, leaders of global mission agencies in the North—including those to whom this book is dedicated—rose to the challenge of developing policies and programs that were more authentically mutual. They asked not only what they might give but what they might receive, not only what they might teach but what and how they might *be* taught. Whether dealing with apartheid in South Africa and Namibia or with an exploitative economic system in the United States or China or Russia, they said, "We in the church need to listen to one another and work with one another." But we need first of all to listen to God's word in Holy Scripture, to the courageous protests of the prophets, and to Saint John's bold claim in the letter of Revelation that God will not allow the oppressive force of the state to be ultimately victorious. We could also do well to take a second look at the legacy of

Luther and his frequently forgotten role against the civil authorities of his day.

Inspired, empowered, and encouraged by the emerging mutuality in mission and informed by the relevancy of Luther's theological legacy, Lutheran leaders and theologians spanning "six continents" have found themselves listening to one another, learning from one another, and celebrating their interdependence as part of the body of Christ in the world.

It is in this light that we wish to acknowledge the helpful role played by a handful of people who have been able, at times with considerable creativity and courage, to listen to what the Spirit is saying to the church during a period of vast historical change. These are the leaders of the global mission units of the ecumenical churches, among them leaders of the ELCA and its predecessor bodies. Backed by dedicated staff and standing committees, these leaders have been willing to alter attitudes and policies, including a deeply entrenched Pietism that has at times contributed to a reluctance to support partner churches to become engaged in social, political, and economic areas of life. It is this group of leaders of the global mission enterprise of our church that has, in recent decades, encouraged and enacted policies to affirm growing self-reliance and confidence on the part of partner churches in the Global South.

It is with gratitude that we dedicate this study book to them.

AIM OF THIS STUDY

As this study book goes to print, an email was received from a pastor who is familiar with all three parts of this series. It is representative of the responses to date: "The *Forgotten Luther* series brings to light one of the best kept secrets of the church. It has inspired me personally and given my congregation the courage to engage in a type of ministry we once considered off-limits. Thank you." Encouraged by many such messages from pastors, deacons, and lay leaders of the church, we have moved with a measure of confidence into the production of this third congregational study book, *The Forgotten Luther III: Reclaiming a Vision of Global Community*.

Congregations are herewith invited, with the help of church leaders and Luther scholars, to consider the new shape of global mission in today's world. Against the growing disparity in wealth, the rising tide of economic refugees, cataclysmic threats to the natural creation, and a pandemic that has brought much of the world to its knees, these essays reflect critically on Luther's oft forgotten social and economic reforms inspired by the central doctrine of justification by grace through faith.

This book will of course prescribe no particular social, political, or economic system or ideology but will seek to lay a foundation on which Christian congregations might find guidance as they reexamine the rationale for their global ministry. Rather, it will ask, within the freedom and discipline of the Christian life, this question: Which systems, structures, or other forms of community life are, at this particular time and place in history, best able to serve the well-being of the whole of God's creation?

Common to the ecumenical church community, this question is reflected in the ELCA's social statement *The Church in Society: A Lutheran Perspective* (1991) as follows: "The witness of this church in society flows from its identity as a community that lives from and for the Gospel. Faith is active in love; love calls for justice in the relationships and structures of society. It is in grateful response to God's grace in Jesus Christ that this church carries out its responsibility for the well-being of society and the environment."[4]

The first study book in this series, *The Forgotten Luther: Reclaiming the Social-Economic Dimension of the Reformation* (Lutheran University Press, 2016), drew our attention to Luther's little-known social and economic reforms, expressed visually in Wittenberg's common chest. The second study book, *The Forgotten Luther II: Reclaiming the Church's Public Witness* (Fortress Press, 2019), challenged the church to raise its voice in the public square as an advocate for the common good.

This third book, *The Forgotten Luther III: Reclaiming a Vision of Global Community*, will draw the *global* implications from Luther's reforms. Together, we will listen to the ways in which churches in the Global South have relied on the Reformation heritage, with its particular insight into the biblical witness, to address the systemic causes of hunger, poverty, and forms of injustice. It is addressed to the whole church at a critical time in history in which vast threats to the environment, a global pandemic, and acute economic hardships are affecting the lives of hundreds of millions of people.

If these essays represent a new way of thinking about our common faith, we ask only that you be open to that. In the face of new challenges, all of us are learning, growing, and exploring ways in which we can be faithful. Debate, question, wrestle with what these presenters are saying, and have a good time. We are saved, not by theology, but by God's grace that we know in Jesus Christ!

---

4. *The Church in Society: A Lutheran Perspective* (Chicago: ELCA, 1991), 1.

ABOUT THE CONTRIBUTORS

Dr. Carter Lindberg

Once again, the Reformation scholar who has inspired this study project calls us to rediscover the Luther who has been forgotten. Claiming that Luther has been relegated to the role of "domestic servant" by the church that bears his name, Lindberg asks simply that we take a second look at how the reformer understood the message of Jesus Christ. Whether because of a pervasive historical amnesia or for reason of the fact that our "lives are imbued with the dogma of competition and a piety of achievement," Christians in North America, claims Lindberg, have a difficult time grasping the radical nature of God's grace, the powerful way this "gospel turns the world upside down." Lindberg makes clear in the initial chapter that in the face of crises, such as a pandemic, acts of genuine Christian charity are natural and largely beneficial. But such acts need to be supplemented by efforts of the civil authorities to address the causes of these crises. Lindberg asks us to look at not only what Luther said and wrote but what he actually *did*, the changes that he instituted in areas of economy, health care, and social security in collaboration with leaders of government. Lindberg's question is to all of us: Is this Luther simply a domestic servant, or is he a prophet of social justice?

Rev. Dr. Ishmael Noko

Few people are more familiar with the crises that affect the global community than former general secretary of the Lutheran World Federation (LWF) Ishmael Noko. A pastor from Zimbabwe with strong global ties, Noko has accompanied southern African churches through their painful but ultimately victorious struggle against systemic racism (apartheid). A signer of the historic 1999 breakthrough agreement—the Joint Declaration on the Doctrine of Justification (JDDJ)—between the Vatican and the churches of the LWF, Noko has also pioneered efforts that draw the concrete implications of this ecumenical consensus for carrying out shared educational, health, and refugee ministry in Africa. While reminding us that Luther is hardly forgotten in the Global South, Noko goes on to ask a penetrating question to churches in the North: Are we not simply perpetuating some of the very practices that Luther railed against?

Rev. Dr. Paul Wee

Having worked with the LWF for twenty-five years, Wee is keenly aware that the Protestant reformer has inspired work in areas of development, mission, study, conflict resolution, and human rights on a global level.

His own work in conflict areas has brought him in contact not only with individuals directly involved but with the economic and political factors that created conflict in the first place. He sets the stage for the third symposium by reviewing the historical origins of Luther's reforms and asking why a major part of the Luther legacy has been forgotten. He goes on to give a brief overview of some areas of the Global South where the economic and political dimension of Christian ministry has been not forgotten but rediscovered with immense vitality.

Rev. Dr. Mitri Raheb

As one of the most articulate leaders of the church in the Global South today, Mitri Raheb asks us to take a second look at the theology of Martin Luther, not from the perspective of scholarship alone, but from the vantage point of real-life struggles. As shooting interrupted his sermons and tanks battered the gates of his parish (Bethlehem's Christmas Lutheran Church in occupied Palestine), Raheb claims to have discovered a much more vibrant and radical edge to his Lutheran beliefs. Dr. Raheb's personal journey through two intifadas (uprisings), the expansion of the State of Israel, and the systematic confiscation of Palestinian land could easily occasion withdrawal, even despair. However, with the help of Luther and a very existential understanding of the Holy Scriptures, of grace, and of hope, Raheb has emerged as a leading voice of churches of the Global South today.

Rev. Dr. Karen L. Bloomquist

Known throughout the global church as an articulate spokesperson for her Luther-inspired critique of the profit economy and the greed that perpetuates it, Bloomquist represents one of the most creative voices in shaping the social policy of the church today. How is the church best equipped to help bring about systemic justice—that is, justice within the systems, structure, policies of community life? Although primarily a theologian and parish pastor, Bloomquist is well acquainted with the workings of global markets, their prime movers as well and their major beneficiaries. She claims that the vast economic polarities created by the global structures of power need to be countered by a gospel-inspired vision of global community. In addition, Bloomquist claims that the new "identity politics," however beneficial in providing certain groups with a sense of belongingness, can ultimately create exclusion. At a critical time in history, she has counsel for pastors, deacons, members of church councils, and laypeople of the church as they work to create genuinely inclusive communities of faith.

Dr. Guillermo Hansen

Coming from a church of the Global South, the Evangelical Lutheran Church of Argentina, Dr. Guillermo Hansen was a young person during a horrific period of the 1970s and 1980s, when the government turned against its own people, "disappearing" some thirty thousand in places of torture and death. It was precisely in this context of violent repression that the "notion of justification by grace through faith prompted in us a new consciousness," he claims. This discovery called forth not only a new way of viewing an article of faith but a whole new way of thinking about life in the world. The global community stands at a historic intersection in world history, claims Hansen, with one road leading to the death of liberal culture, the other to the revitalization of a democracy based on values of equity, justice, and the care of creation. For people of faith, this is a time of decision.

Rev. Dr. Rafael Malpica Padilla

Asking to build the critically important bridge between the forgotten Luther, the global mission movement, and the life of the parish is Rafael Malpica Padilla. Few are better equipped for this task. Lutheran theologian Paul Tillich once noted that the best place to acquire knowledge is on the boundary—that is, the meeting place between traditions, worldviews, nations, cultures, and the like. The truth in Tillich's remark is borne out in Malpica Padilla's life and ministry. With one foot in the South and one in the North, one in the ecumenical world and one in the Lutheran tradition, one in the developing world and one in the developed, Malpica Padilla brings critical experience and knowledge to bear on the shape of the mission of the global church in today's world. As director of the Global Mission unit of the Evangelical Lutheran Church in America (ELCA), he is particularly well suited to the question of how the local congregation can be better equipped to engage the challenge of a revitalized global mission today.

1.

The Immigrant Luther

Domestic Servant or Prophet of Social Justice?

CARTER LINDBERG

The recently concluded European "decade of the Reformation" put Martin Luther on the global stage. Yet Luther remains an immigrant in the United States. We'll return to this in a moment, but first, a few notes on the global Luther.

The globalization of Luther was a marketing success of the five hundredth anniversary of the Reformation that ranged from tourism and exhibitions to Playmobil Luthers and other kitsch. Such commercial "Luther lite," however, conveniently ignores his excoriation of unjust economic realities, prophetic critiques of political overreach, and creative moves for social justice.[1]

Of course, almost from the outset of Luther's career, he became a mass media sensation thanks to his linguistic skills, the printing press, and the illustrative genius of his artist friend Lucas Cranach.[2] Luther's Latin writings gained a broad learned audience, but Luther chose also to write in German "for the laity," and that popular move was imitated in vernacular translations throughout and beyond Europe. Luther's emphasis on the vernacular is an important step toward global Christianity, a point highlighted by the late scholar of African Christianity Lamin Sanneh: "Christianity is a translated religion without a revealed language. . . . Without translation there would be no Christianity or Christians. Translation is the

---

1. See Carter Lindberg, "Luther on the Market Economy," *LQ* 30, no. 4 (2016): 373–92; Carter Lindberg and Paul Wee, eds., *The Forgotten Luther: Reclaiming the Social-Economic Dimension of the Reformation* (Minneapolis: Lutheran University Press, 2016); and Ryan Cumming, ed., *The Forgotten Luther II: Reclaiming the Church's Public Witness* (Minneapolis: Fortress, 2019).

2. See Andrew Pettegree, *Brand Luther: 1517, Printing, and the Making of the Reformation* (New York: Penguin, 2015).

church's birthmark as well as its missionary benchmark: the church would be unrecognizable or unsustainable without it."[3] So, for example, Luther's colleague Philip Melanchthon translated the Augsburg Confession into Greek and sent it to Patriarch Jeremias of the Greek Orthodox Church, and Luther was visited by an Ethiopian Christian, Michael the Deacon.[4] In our time, the "globalization" of Luther is manifest in translations of his writings into every major world language. Scholarly societies for Luther studies exist throughout the world, and scholars from every continent participate in the International Congress for Luther Research events.

Does any of this extensive global study of Luther and the Reformation filter down to Lutheran theological education, let alone parishes? I suspect very little. Many Lutherans, like most Americans, are amnesiacs with regard to origins and how we got this way. A terrible thing about amnesia is loss of identity. Without knowing who we are, we are prone to accept popular reconstructions of our identity, such as Michael Massing erroneously proposes in his recent book *Fatal Discord: Erasmus, Luther, and the Fight for the Western Mind*, which presents Luther as a zealot pioneering the American Evangelical Right.[5]

If we forget how radical Luther's proclamation of the gospel really is, we are susceptible to such value judgments. I want to emphasize this because our culture's ideology of self-justification is even more "medieval" than Luther's context. Our lives are imbued with the dogma of competition and a piety of achievement. Wolfgang Greive writes, "It is significant that the modern experience of works righteousness is uninterrupted. Nurture and forgiveness are foreign words; constant [self-]justification finds no grace. This is the origin of the 'sacrament of work,' the 'performance cult,' the 'scandal of unemployment' and the spreading feeling 'Am I still needed.'"[6] We measure our worth by our success in self-actualization. Sure, we Lutherans still talk a lot about "grace alone," but we tend to live by the axiom "There's no free lunch." Well, of course, there is; it's called the Lord's Supper. There are no ifs, ands, or buts here in the gospel. As Luther affirmed, you are named in God's last will and testament; God

3. Lamin Sanneh cited in Viggo Mortensen, "From Confessional Ecumenics to Theology of Religions," in *Europäisches und globales christentum / European and Global Christianity*, ed. Katharina Kunter and Jens Holger Schjørring (Göttingen, Germany: Vandenhoeck and Ruprecht, 2011), 354–73, 362n12.

4. George Mastrantonis, *Augsburg and Constantinople: The Correspondence between the Tübingen Theologians and Patriarch Jeremiah II of Constantinople on the Augsburg Confession* (Brookline, MA: Holy Orthodox Press, 1982); David D. Daniels III and Lawrence Anglin, "Luther and the Ethiopian Deacon," *LQ* 32, no. 4 (2018): 428–34.

5. Michael Massing, *Fatal Discord: Erasmus, Luther, and the Fight for the Western Mind* (New York: HarperCollins, 2018).

6. Wolfgang Greive, ed., "Hermeneutics of the Indicative," in *Justification in the World's Context* (Geneva: Lutheran World Federation, 2000), 229–39, 234.

has died, so God's will is in effect. You receive the inheritance![7] Luther emphasizes the good news of the "happy exchange" of Christ's righteousness with your sin: "Lord, Jesus, you are my righteousness, just as I am your sin. You have taken upon yourself what is mine and given to me what is yours." The corollary is this: "Beware of aspiring to such purity that you will not wish to be looked upon as a sinner, or to be one. For Christ dwells only in sinners."[8]

In short, the only prerequisite to God's grace is sin, and we all qualify! As Luther wrote to Melanchthon, "If you are a preacher of grace, then preach a true and not a fictitious grace; if grace is true, you must bear a true and not a fictitious sin. God does not save people who are only fictitious sinners. Be a sinner and sin boldly, for he is victorious over sin, death, and the world."[9] A problem for our culture, of course, is that sin has become a fiction, but "without Luther's understanding of sin, theology deteriorates into moralism."[10] That's why Luther's definition of theology is so important: "The proper subject of theology is man guilty of sin and condemned, and God the Justifier and Savior of man the sinner. Whatever is asked or discussed in theology outside this subject, is error and poison."[11]

As real sinners, we can rejoice that salvation is received, not achieved! There are no closed gates to the city of God! That "Mighty Fortress" is wide open—the good news for all of us pilgrims and strangers in a foreign land is that there are no rivers to swim, no walls to climb, no documents to show in order to enter the kingdom. No matter what your color, origin, or language, you are accepted. In the words of Eric Gritsch and Robert Jenson, "The gospel tolerates no conditions. It is itself unconditional promise. . . . This is the first and fundamental Lutheran proposal of dogma. When it is practiced consistently, the Lutheran Reformation has succeeded, whatever else may happen."[12] The gospel's unconditional promise delivers us from what Luther calls the "monster of uncertainty," that introspection of both medieval and modern piety that is constantly feeling our spiritual pulses to see if we are acceptable to God—or, more likely, to our culture and its idols. So Luther asserts, "This is the reason why our theology is

7. "A Treatise on the New Testament, That Is, the Holy Mass," 1520, in *LW* 35:75–111, 88. See "The Babylonian Captivity of the Church," 1520, in *LW* 36:3–126, 38; and "Church Postil," 1544, in *LW* 79:47–48.

8. "To Georg Spenlein," 1516, in *LW* 48:11–14, 12–13. See Martin Luther, "The Freedom of a Christian," 1520, in *LW* 31:327–77, 351–53.

9. "To Philip Melanchthon," 1521, in *LW* 48:277–82, 281–82.

10. Gerhard Ebeling, "Luther and the Beginning of the Modern Age," in *Luther and the Dawn of the Modern Era*, ed. Heiko A. Oberman (Leiden: Brill, 1974), 11–39, 39.

11. "Commentary on Psalm 51," 1538, in *LW* 12:311.

12. Eric W. Gritsch and Robert W. Jenson, *Lutheranism: The Theological Movement and Its Confessional Writings* (Philadelphia: Fortress, 1976), 44.

certain: it snatches us away from ourselves and places us outside ourselves, so that we do not depend on our own strength, conscience, experience, person, or works but depend on that which is outside ourselves, that is, on the promise and truth of God, which cannot deceive."[13]

The ramifications of this gospel were almost immediately spelled out in new social-economic programs that moved beyond the self-aggrandizement of medieval charity and the higher hedonism of modern philanthropy to communal tax-supported institutions foreshadowing the modern socialism of Germany and the Nordic countries. The gospel turns the world upside down: the first shall be last, and the last shall be first. It reflects Mary's song that the rich and powerful shall be overturned, the song that became the basis for Luther's advice to his prince.[14] Luther placed the common good over personal gain and advocated for and helped create legislation for government programs for universal education, support of the unemployed and underemployed, and universal affordable health care.[15] The gospel, in short, is provocative—it calls forth, it incites, it challenges; it also provokes, irritates, and angers. It inspires service to the local and global neighbor and challenges those who would withhold or privatize such service. Indeed, the gospel is so provocative that our usual gambit is to domesticate the messenger.

The history of the interpretation of Luther reveals the same move to domesticate the messenger and thus the message as that which replaces the crucified Christ with a sweet, otherworldly Jesus and discipleship with a prosperity gospel. Luther is domesticated into the pantheon of great men of history. Luther is the German Hercules; the hero of the German people; and insofar as he comes to America, the ideal German American and, according to Massing, the stimulus for the Second Great Awakening and American individualism.[16] In 1884, a year after the four hundredth anniversary of Luther's birth, a replica of the Worms, Germany, statue of Luther erected before Memorial Lutheran Church in Washington, DC, "was supposed to represent the best qualities of the Teutonic character [faith in progress and liberty], shared by Americans and Germans." And in 1936, a similar Luther statue erected in Baltimore "was meant as a demonstration of German national pride, of pride renewed after the disaster of 1917/18. During the ceremony, the

13. "Lectures on Galatians," 1535, in *LW* 26:387.

14. See my "Reclaiming Luther's Public Witness on Church, State, and War," in Cumming, *Forgotten Luther II*, 7–24.

15. See my "Luther and the Common Chest," in Lindberg and Wee, *Forgotten Luther*, 17–29; and Wolfgang Huber, "Worldly Worship: The Reformation and Economic Ethics," in *The Protestant Reformation of the Church and the World*, ed. John Witte Jr. and Amy Wheeler (Louisville, KY: Westminster John Knox, 2018), 161–77.

16. Massing, *Fatal Discord*, 819–20.

persecution of those disciples of Luther in Germany who were not ready to follow Hitler's commands, was deliberately ignored."[17]

We like to make important figures in our image. So Luther becomes the supporter of our cause. Such "great man" theories of history reveal more about the times than the subject. Examples include "from Luther to Bismarck," "from Luther to Hitler," and now "from Luther to Trump."[18] These appeals to Luther are often expressions of populism, nativism, and racism. So, for example, in the wake of the Napoleonic Wars, German resentment of all things French (and, by extension, all things southern European and Roman Catholic) spilled over into traditional American nativist and populist suspicion of Catholic immigrants, who were characterized as lazy, immoral, and untrustworthy—in brief, as archenemies of the American "Way of Life."[19]

In stark contrast to these typical depictions of Luther, there is the predella of the 1547 Cranach altarpiece in Wittenberg, Germany, that depicts Luther in the pulpit. Here Luther does not face us in a heroic gaze but looks and points to Christ on the cross, the crucified but living Christ. The central subject is not Luther but Christ. In contrast to medieval predellas that depict Christ horizontally and dead, this image of "the living Christ in Wittenberg literally subverts tradition, turning it ninety degrees. The dead, horizontal Christ is now vertical and alive, rejecting pictorial tradition and defining the Wittenberg community."[20]

A more recent contrast to typical presentations of Luther is *Table Talk with Luther*, the life-size triptych by Uwe Pfeifer commissioned by the Martin Luther University of Halle-Wittenberg for the 1983 East German joint commemoration of Marx (1818–83) and Luther (1483–1546).[21] The center panel places Luther at a table in a radio or television studio with twentieth-century men and women. The microphones are directed to Luther. Opposite Luther is a dark-skinned man in combat fatigues (possibly recalling images of Che Guevara), his machine pistol draped across the back of his chair and his wristwatch showing five to twelve. What are

17. Hartmut Lehmann, "The Reformation and America: The Luther Statues in Washington and Baltimore," in *Die Reformation in Deutschland und Amerika: Interpretationen und Debatten*, ed. Hans Guggisberg and Gottfried Krodel (Gütersloh, Germany: Gütersloher, 1993), 647–64, 664.

18. See, for example, Hartmut Lehmann, *Luthergedächtnis 1817 bis 2017* (Göttingen, Germany: Vandenhoeck and Ruprecht, 2012); and Michael Massing, "How Martin Luther Paved the Way for Donald Trump," *Nation*, April 19, 2018, https://tinyurl.com/y3klb8u7.

19. Lehmann, *Luthergedächtnis*, 39; Hartmut Lehmann, "Demythologizing the Luther Myths 1883–1983," *LQ* 30, no. 4 (2016): 410–29, 426; Paul A. Baglyos, "American Lutherans at the Dawn of the Republic," *LQ* 13, no. 1 (1999): 51–74, 61–62.

20. Bonnie Noble, *Lucas Cranach the Elder: Art and Devotion of the German Reformation* (Lanham, MD: University Press of America, 2009), 116.

21. Jutta Strehle, *Martin Luther 1983: Lutherinterpretation in der bildenden Kunst der ehemaligen DDR* (Griesheim, Germany: Bassenauer, 1992), 54–55.

they discussing? War? Terrorism? Economic oppression? What does the watch mean? The nuclear clock? Climate crisis? An actual chair is placed before the triptych so that we can join the conversation. Here Luther is not a past hero endorsing our views but a global conversation partner with the present. That's dangerous, of course, so East Germany decided the triptych too controversial to be displayed. Meanwhile, the East German churches continued to host prayer and discussion meetings, which led to mass nonviolent demonstrations and the destruction of that wall separating the country.

Have the American Lutheran churches forgotten this Luther? The proclaimer of the gospel who challenged the religious, social, and political establishments? The Luther who held up Mary's song to his prince as the reminder that the rich shall be sent hungry away and the powerful cast down? About a century ago, a satire appeared titled *Little Journeys with Martin Luther*, "in which the American replica of the Worms statue . . . came to life and Martin Luther stalked the United States in search of a place where his teaching was still alive—and, predictably, found none."[22] From colonial days, Luther has been a foreigner in America. The dominance of English Puritanism supplemented by continental Pietism and enflamed by revivalism left Luther in the lurch. In the enthusiasm of revivalism, "religion prospered while theology slowly went bankrupt."[23] Philip Schaff (1819–93), "the Father of American Church History," wrote to German colleagues, "[Americanized Lutheran] preachers . . . are much more concerned about building programs and politics than theology and church affairs."[24] Conditions seem not to have improved by the time Dietrich Bonhoeffer visited Union Seminary in 1930–31, for he noted that American Protestantism lacked the Reformation.[25] Similarly, George W. Forell, who escaped National Socialism and attended the Lutheran seminary in Philadelphia, was surprised by the conservative Pietism of his teachers.[26] Forell later suggested that American studies of Luther reflected an immigrant Lutheran concern to build churches and that Luther was honored but not studied.[27] Karl Hertz was more direct: "The strongest influence in the

22. Jaroslav Pelikan, "Luther Comes to the New World," in Oberman, *Dawn of the Modern Era*, 1–10, 3.

23. Henry Steele Commager, *The American Mind: An Interpretation of American Thought and Character since The 1880s* (New Haven, CT: Yale University Press, 1950), 165.

24. Quoted in Carl Meyer, ed., *Moving Frontiers: Readings in the History of the Lutheran Church-Missouri Synod* (St. Louis, MO: Concordia, 1964), 185.

25. See Helmut Edelmann, *Dem Glauben ein Gesicht geben*, vol. 6, *Lutherisch? Lutheran?* (Husum, Germany: Matthiesen Verlag, 2017), 124–45.

26. George W. Forell, "Theology in Exile: A Personal Account," *LQ* 29, no. 3 (2015): 304–11.

27. George W. Forell, "Lutherforschung in den USA," in *Lutherforschung Heute. Referate und Berichte des 1. Internationalen Lutherforschungskongresses*, ed. Vilmos Vajta (Berlin: Lutherisches Verlagshaus, 1958), 137–45.

shaping of American Lutheranism in my judgment has been Pietism."
The consequence was "a more quietistic, personalistic ethic."[28] A major
source for immigrant piety was Johann Arndt (1555–1621), whose *Four
Books on True Christianity* (1610) became the classical devotional text
for Protestantism, with a circulation second only to the Bible.[29] The title
itself indicates Pietism's direction toward an "adjectival," "interiorized"
Christianity with faith described as "true," "living," "heartfelt," and "expe-
riential." Arndt came to America in the hearts and luggage of Lutheran
immigrants. Lutheran Pietism conceded Luther's crucial role in initiating the Reformation but criticized him for not emphasizing holy living.

It is easy to caricature Pietism as moralistic—no card playing, games,
dancing, or jokes and a gray seriousness well depicted in the movie *Babette's
Feast*. But there are grounds for such caricatures in August Hermann
Francke (1663–1727), the genius behind the influential institutions in Halle
and a source for the so-called Protestant ethic. His "Rules for Living"[30]
condemned laziness and stressed hard work and obedience to authority as
the means to and fruit of godliness. Pietism was suspicious of the world
and emphasized conversion, rebirth, and sanctification of the individual as
the keys to changing society. Pietism's emphasis on the religious virtues
of industriousness, thrift, and obedience to authority strongly influenced
bourgeois ethics. Halle Pietism became a kind of Prussian state religion.[31]

In contrast to such spiritual athleticism, Luther insisted "that the spiritual life had to be lived in the world . . . with all its endless difficulties
and frustrations." As Hans Hillerbrand describes it, "Lutheran spirituality
begins and ends with the celebration of the mundane, the ordinary life as
the vehicle for glorifying God" in the multifaceted vocation of the Christian.[32] Vocation is "worship in the realm of the world."[33] As Luther once
admonished Melanchthon, "We are to be men and not God."[34] Following
Luther, Berndt Hamm suggests, "Where God takes people into his service
as saints he does not lead them into fenced-off, sanctified reserves but

28. Karl Hertz, "The Two Kingdoms Debate—a Look at the American Situation," in
Lutheran Churches—Salt or Mirror of Society?, ed. Ulrich Duchrow (Geneva: Lutheran World
Federation, 1977), 243–54, 245.
29. See Johannes Wallmann, "Johann Arndt (1555–1621)," in *The Pietist Theologians*, ed.
Carter Lindberg (Oxford: Blackwell, 2005), 21–37.
30. See Georg Helbig, ed., *August Hermann Francke, Lebensregeln* (Marburg, Germany:
Francke Buchhandlung, 1983).
31. See Richard L. Gawthrop, *Pietism and the Making of Eighteenth-Century Prussia* (Cambridge: Cambridge University Press, 1993).
32. Hans J. Hillerbrand, "The Road Less Traveled? Reflections on the Enigma of Lutheran
Spirituality," in *Let Christ Be Christ*, ed. Daniel N. Harmelink (Huntington Beach, CA: Ten-
tatio, 1999), 129–40, 134, 138, 140.
33. Vilmos Vajta, *Die Theologie des Gottesdienstes bei Luther* (Stockholm: Svenska Kyrkans
Diakonistyrelses Bokförlag, 1952), 314.
34. "To George Spalatin," 1530, in *LW* 49:337.

into the everyday areas of work, politics, family and neighborhood, enabling them to become active witnesses of his self-giving love in the midst of the unholy world."[35] In his "Treatise on Good Works," Luther wrote, "Look, there are plenty of good works to be done! Most of the mighty, most of the rich, and most of [their] friends are unjust and exercise their power over the poor, the lowly, and over their opponents. The more powerful they are, the worse their deeds. And where one cannot prevent this by force and help the truth, one can at least confess the truth and do something for it by our words, not the kind which please the unrighteous or agree with them, but those which speak the truth boldly."[36]

In a startling departure from both medieval and modern understandings of piety, Luther wrote, "If mercy is this abundant, then there is no holiness in us. Then it is a fictitious expression to speak of a 'holy man,' just as it is a fictitious expression to speak of God's falling into sin; for by the nature of things, this cannot be. . . . Those whom we call 'holy' are made holy by an alien holiness, through Christ, by the holiness of free mercy. . . . Therefore let us keep quiet about holiness and holy people."[37] Sharply put, "It is not the proper role of the gospel to make people pious but rather only to make Christians. To be a Christian is quite simply to be pious. A person may be pious without being Christian."[38] Luther warns against "too much religion" lest we "lose Christ."[39] A person's "piety" is no more a personal achievement than is justification.[40]

"Too much religion" but no Christ! What is that in our context other than the civil religion that blithely "baptizes" American exceptionalism? Protestantism without Reformation has nurtured an American self-righteous, nationalistic identification with the kingdom of God, and the Pietist concern for mission to the world has been secularized into a triumphalistic crusade to impose American interests on the world. Pietism in America has become decadent.[41]

Luther "unbound" from the secularized pieties of civil religion may provide resources for addressing current American and global challenges. This, however, entails our responsibility to remember—to remember not the myths and monuments to Luther that endorse our issues but rather Luther's provocative proclamation of the gospel. Luther wanted to be judged by his teaching, not his person, saying, "I ask that men

35. Berndt Hamm, *The Reformation of Faith in the Context of Late Medieval Theology and Piety*, ed. Robert J. Bast (Leiden: Brill, 2004), 281–82.

36. "Treatise on Good Works," 1520, in *LW* 44:51.

37. "Commentary on Psalm 51," 1538, in *LW* 12:324–25.

38. Sermon on Matt 9:18–26, in *WA* 10/1.2:430, 30–32.

39. "Commentary on Psalm 51," 1538, in *LW* 12:352.

40. Sermon on Matt 21:1–9, in *WA* 10/1.2:36, 4–8.

41. See Gerhard Forde, "Radical Lutheranism," *LQ* 1, no. 1 (1987): 5–18.

make no reference to my name; let them call themselves Christians, not Lutherans."[42] So Luther enjoined his followers to say, "Whether Luther is a rascal or a saint I do not care; his teaching is not his, but Christ's."[43]

We have a responsibility to remember past resources for the present proclamation of the gospel. There is much in Luther's teaching that directly addresses us and our times; to remember this is not antiquarianism. As Jaroslav Pelikan observed, "Tradition is the living faith of the dead; traditionalism is the dead faith of the living."[44] Our tradition provides a horizon to get our bearings and chart our course. Even novice sailors know it is foolish to navigate by sighting the prow rather than by sighting land or the stars. Our tradition is a resource for responding to contemporary issues by liberating us from that presentism that does not see beyond its nose.

Our forerunners in the faith shook the foundations of their cultures precisely because they knew that God's promise allows us to be responsible. Luther's constructive response to social injustice and political oppression did not begin with social-political activity but with preaching. He remembered what we often forget: the first word is what God has done for us, and the second word is what we can do for others. He said, "A Christian is a perfectly free lord of all, subject to none. A Christian is a perfectly dutiful servant of all, subject to all."[45] In recalling his struggle with the papists, Luther wrote, "I opposed indulgences and the papists, but never with force. I simply taught, preached, and wrote God's Word; otherwise I did nothing. And while I slept . . . or drank Wittenberg beer with my friends Philip and Amsdorf, the Word so greatly weakened the papacy that no prince or emperor ever inflicted such losses upon it, I did nothing; the Word did everything."[46] "The Word did everything"—that is worth remembering.

STUDY QUESTIONS

1. Why do you think Luther's teachings might be important for us to hear again today?
2. Lindberg quotes Hans J. Hillerbrand, who cites Luther as writing, "Lutheran spirituality begins and ends with the celebration

42. "A Sincere Admonition by Martin Luther to All Christians to Guard against Insurrection and Rebellion," 1522, in *LW* 45:70–71.

43. "Receiving Both Kinds in the Sacrament," 1522, in *LW* 36:265.

44. Jaroslav Pelikan, *The Christian Tradition: A History of the Development of Doctrine*, vol. 1, *The Emergence of the Catholic Tradition* (Chicago: University of Chicago Press, 1975), 9.

45. Luther, "Freedom of a Christian," 31:344.

46. "Eight Sermons at Wittenberg," 1522, in *LW* 51:77.

of the mundane, the ordinary life as the vehicle for glorifying God." What do you think it means to "celebrate the mundane"?

3. How might remembering that we are sinners saved by grace help motivate the church to work for justice in the world?

4. Thinking of Lindberg's critique of Pietism, where do you see Pietism at work today?

2.

Reclaiming a Vision of Global Community

ISHMAEL NOKO

The idea that Martin Luther is "forgotten" does not pass my reality check. This will be true also for other Protestant Christians from the Global South for the simple reason that the intensive work of the Lutheran World Federation (LWF)—in advocacy, refugee assistance, education, medical and health programs, missiology, chaplaincies of different kinds, and ecumenical dialogues that lead to the pulpit and altar fellowship—is relevant in their lives today. Lutheran churches within the various nations are involved in programs similar to the ones mentioned in relation to the work of the LWF as a global communion of churches.

These churches are far from entertaining the thought that Luther is forgotten. For them, such a theme or topic at face value would be left to the academic community. The simple reason would be that academics are perceived as having lots of time at their disposal to the extent that they can chase a "monkey without a tail," hoping to catch it. The rest of the ordinary men and women are focused on juggling social problems such as unemployment and poverty. They will not concern themselves too much with academic and theological jargon. They believe in the Martin Luther they encounter when studying and meditating on the Small Catechism. To them, Luther is that pedagogist who constantly poses a critical question—*What does this mean?* It is this probing question that enables them to make sense of challenges encountered daily in the marketplaces of life.

IMPORTANCE OF THE SMALL CATECHISM

Luther is supposed to have encouraged his contemporaries and coworkers to not preserve his literary works except for the Small Catechism and his letter to his theological opponent Desiderius Erasmus, a Dutch humanist philosopher whose views on the Eucharist Luther opposed very strongly. Luther's Small Catechism rose in importance over decades as a text for explaining the biblical message of salvation and as a resource for preachers and family devotions. When read against and within the context of the multireligious and multicultural societies, it served and continues to serve as one of the best pastoral documents for Christian education and theological education to this day. This is due in part because the rhythm of life in ancient times in southern Africa was organized around very strict, must-be-kept religious rituals. Compliance by the religious community representative or individual with the guidelines was imperative; otherwise, life would be disrupted, allowing negative forces to destroy the normalcy of human life. Salvation in traditional religions was therefore dependent on *good works* linked to human compliance. God's grace manifested in good life, and prosperity was therefore a consequence of good actions by human beings. Luther's theological and pastoral contribution in this context of traditional societies is his emphasis on justification by faith alone.

The fundamental difference(s) between Christian theology and the theologies of other Indigenous religious traditions in southern Africa is a question of theoanthropology. This revolves around issues of how God and human beings may interact and how human beings may participate in the divine salvation process. Luther's punctuating cry, "How can I get a gracious God?" is central to the fundamental difference between Christian theology and the traditional theologies. Luther's call reflects a person searching for God and not finding salvation within his or her own resourcefulness. For this very reason, Luther's Small Catechism is an invaluable and impeccable response not only to the existential question about human salvation asked by every religious formation but also to the relevance of Luther's thoughts to this day. In other words, the Small Catechism is an important resource for Christian formation.

LUTHER IN THE GLOBAL CONTEXT OF HIS TIME

In the 1990s, I was invited by the founder of the Amity Foundation, Bishop K. H. Ting, to mainland China to be among the witnesses when a Chinese translation of a book on the life of Luther, *Here I Stand* by Roland Bainton, was launched. This book forms the basis of a series of lectures by a Chinese professor—Chang Chi Pang from Singapore—sponsored then by the LWF. Such a publication demonstrates that even though we may not identify Luther, his thoughts and his basic message continue to influence people and communities in different cultures and settings. Even though Luther chose to stand back, and may not be identifiable, his thoughts and teachings nonetheless continue to influence people and communities in different cultures and settings.

From historical records, we get the impression that Luther did not travel much beyond the Germany of his time. But that is not to say that he lacked a global view! For instance, we know that he received delegations from all over Europe, from England, Constantinople, and Africa. Luther was a monk of the Augustinian order, based on the teachings of Saint Augustine of Hippo, an African, and so could be assumed to be sensitive to the world outside medieval Europe. In 1534, Luther met Michael the Deacon, a cleric of the Ethiopian Orthodox Church. Their dialogue produced interesting results. Michael affirmed the Augsburg Confession, while Luther stated that the Mass used by the Ethiopian Orthodox Church is compatible with the Lutheran Mass.

Tradition has it also that Luther received students from West Africa who participated in his regular table talks in Wittenberg. He commented on current affairs such as wars involving Turkey, which speaks well of his knowledge of the outside world. From these contacts, his understanding of the catholicity of the church as one, holy, Catholic, and apostolic was certainly deepened.

In 1520, Luther wrote an open letter to the "Christian Nobility of the German Nation." This letter is one of the significant milestones in the development of the Protestant Reformation. Luther and his coreformers in Wittenberg realized at that moment that the point of no return with regard to the struggle with Rome had been reached. The next logical step had to be the unfortunate but necessary tragedy of breaking all connections with Rome. This letter by Luther awakened the political authorities, the church, and the Christian laity in a persuasive but biblically based argumentation regarding their role in shaping the future of the church and society in Germany. In the letter, he attacks the papacy and its claim of supremacy over temporal and spiritual spheres.

This letter gave the laity control over their own faith and detracted control from the papacy and the church. The statement that everyone is a priest, that everyone should base their faith on their own interpretation of the Scriptures, shocked not only the established church but also other reformers. This was the beginning of a new reformation based on accessible Scripture that every Christian was able to interpret. It also opened the door for individuals to get involved in the governance of the affairs of the church and society, which would influence political developments over the coming centuries.

Luther argued that the doctrine of purgatory and the payment of indulgences had no basis in Scripture. Indulgences were meant to obtain the release of souls from purgatory, where they might have languished because they died without receiving the last rites during, for example, the black death and the Crusades. Priests were paid to pray for the souls of these dead, to obtain their release. Luther pointed out that Christ died for the world (John 3:16), and therefore, there is no need or justification for indulgences, since we are set free on the basis of faith in Christ and the grace of God. This is the concept of justification that Luther saw as the one and firm rock, the chief article of the whole Christian doctrine, on which the actual witness of the church shall stand or fall.

Against the globalist background of Luther's vision, some of his utterances about Jews and Turks were, to say the least, deplorable. His remarks on the Jewish people have had long-lasting, damaging consequences for Christian-Jewish relations. Ideologies such as Nazism benefitted from such statements. Lutheran churches within the LWF distanced themselves in 1984 from these statements without, however, denying or demonizing Luther.[1]

Similarly, the Evangelical Church in Germany said, on the five hundredth anniversary of Luther's birth, "We state clearly that through omission and silence, we too have become guilty before the Merciful God of the outrage perpetrated against the Jews by members of our (German) people."[2]

The above reactions of Lutheran churches and organizations showed that they understood that such remarks would undermine international relations and the promotion of the vision of a global community—the very vision Luther propagated. Mutual understanding requires the overcoming of enemy images and the lack of respect for one another, the demobilizing of the anathemas of one another, and developing a vocabulary to express the vision of a global community. To me, this means that the message of Luther remains relevant. He was not an infallible being. He left behind a vision that can self-correct, that can identify aspects that undermine the greater vision of a global community that builds a better society.

LUTHER IN THE ECUMENICAL CONTEXT

Luther never intended to have a church named after him. He understood that the church, as confessed in the creeds, is the body of Christ. For that reason, he believed that the church was one even though it was experiencing structural fragmentation. Therefore, the division of the church in the sixteenth century was a tragedy but a necessary one that was intended

---

1. "A Shift in Jewish-Lutheran Relations? (Documentation 48)," Lutheran World Federation, 2003, https://tinyurl.com/g3k1peyx.

2. "Christians and Jews: A Manifesto 50 Years after the Weissensee Declaration," Evangelical Church in Germany, November 9, 2000, https://tinyurl.com/2ndm7cpk.

to recover the gospel message of justification. The Lutheran identity was marked by ecumenical initiatives seeking renewal and the recovery of the gospel and the unity of the church. Therefore, in recent years, ecumenical conversations and dialogues between the Lutheran churches and the Roman Catholic Church led to the Joint Declaration on the Doctrine of Justification (JDDJ), signed in 1999 in Augsburg, Germany, by representatives of the LWF and the Roman Catholic Church. This multilateral ecumenical agreement bears the potential of common witness among churches. The idea behind the joint declaration was and is the promotion of unity for the purpose of reconciling the body of Christ. The Apostles' Creed, which is recited every Sunday, says, "I believe in one, holy, catholic, and apostolic church." Not a divided church. The concept of a global church as envisioned by Luther lies at the foundation of the JDDJ. The church families that subscribe to the JDDJ (Lutherans, Roman Catholics, Anglicans, Reformed, Presbyterians, Methodists) count nearly two billion adherents—a truly global community. This is a great opportunity for the churches in dialogue to share ecclesial insights.

Another example of the voice of Luther finding expression can be found in the document *From Conflict to Communion*. This document was signed and exchanged in the year 2017 before Pope Francis and his cardinals and the president of the LWF and his council. It recognizes that the two church partners are committed to working together toward the realization of the gift of communion. On the same occasion, the diaconal agencies of the two churches signed a partnership agreement committing their organizations to act together in addressing social and justice issues such as poverty, refugee advocacy, and protecting the environment.

For the first time in five hundred years, there is agreement among churches that were divided on the understanding of the doctrine of justification. This matter pertains not only to Lutherans and Roman Catholics, but it is an important teaching for the universal church of Jesus Christ: that justification is received through accepting the grace of God in Christ through faith and that personal merit is the fruit of faith.

The joint declaration provided a consensus, a solid basis for the common understanding of the doctrine of justification between the leaders of more than two billion believers worldwide. Now that these common points of understanding have been identified, the outstanding arguments will be easier to resolve, including the relationship between the word of God and church doctrine and the relationship between justification and social ethics.

Such a global community of like-minded people can have an enormous impact on issues such as the disparity of income in the world and the development of healthy and ethical communities, truly the embodiment of the expression "the salt of the earth" (Matt 5:13–16). Together, we can, in the words of the joint declaration, "deepen our common understanding of justification and make it bear fruit in the life and teachings of the churches."[3]

This feels like a transition in the argument taking place here—do you need a header such as "Luther and Social Justice Today"?

In remembering the "forgotten Luther" and the equitable community he inspired, we need to look at the massive indebtedness of poor countries to rich countries and ask ourselves, Are these not the practices Luther preached against? Are these not the modern usurers he despised? We should note actions like that of Norway, which, a few years ago, canceled the debt of developing countries, and Ecuador, which undertook an audit of its debt to determine the legitimacy thereof.

Luther did address in a critical manner the creation and management of wealth. Hence he developed in Wittenberg a common chest. In his time, the concept of usury was important, and he saw wealth as a gift that must be used wisely and equitably and to the benefit of the wider society. In this spirit, we should note the actions, in our time, of wealthy individuals who transferred their enormous personal wealth, bigger than the economies of several small countries, to benevolent foundations. Lutheran churches and members of the World Council of Churches are using their opportunities of engagement with governments to apply their Christian principles and Protestant ethics to influence polities toward more equitable sharing of resources and preferential treatment for weaker members of their societies.

I would argue that Luther has not been forgotten, except in the manner in which the organizers of the conference stated. Nonetheless, his thoughts and his voice have not been silenced, especially bearing in mind that the Reformation of the sixteenth century was a reformation not just of the church but of society as a whole. For that reason, we need not be surprised when secular voices articulate the concerns that Luther was all about on this matter of economics. The social movements and activists of today derive their strength from the thoughts of people like Luther, Ulrich Zwingli, and other reformers. The social and economic implications of the gospel proclaimed by the reformers independent of those who sowed it led to concern for social change and to the concept of the UN, a global community of nations. This global sentiment is found also, for example, in letters from heads of churches and organizations addressed to heads of states and governments on social and political issues such as apartheid and the situations in Venezuela, Zimbabwe, and the Middle East. These

---

3. Lowell G. Almen, "Joint Declaration on Justification: History Making or Precious Memory?," *Journal of Lutheran Ethics* 9, no. 10 (2009): para. 43, https://www.elca.org/JLE/Articles/354.

are but expressions of the voice of Luther and others that have not been forgotten but continue to influence the conscience of nations.

Lutherans worldwide realized that a decent global community is marked by social, economic, and political interdependency. Such interdependency is imperative for the social good, benefiting members of society equally. Further, it is marked by equity and the provision of education, health care, fresh water, care for the aged, children and mother prioritization, and rights of women. The LWF has programs to support the First Nations; environmental projects such as the planting of trees in Mauritania, Africa; and advocacy for peace in the Middle East, to mention a few.

The social good enables governments, citizens, private businesses, and industry to collaborate for mutual progress of the human family and for the health of this planet, our common home. It is therefore important that every civil society and religious community confront its past without hesitation in order to learn from history. The mistakes and sins of the past should not stand in the way of the creation of a global community. In its ecumenical engagement, the LWF has sought to deal with its own past in relation to other worldwide church families, such as the Anabaptists and Roman Catholics as indicated in the JDDJ.

CONCLUSION

Luther and the other reformers led a movement of new thinking, challenging the political, social, and economic structures of their times. Coupled with the new technology of the day—the printing press—this challenge created a profoundly destabilizing disruption of society. We can deduce the shock of Luther and his fellow reformers at public violence such as the Peasants' War of 1524. This uprising of hundreds of thousands of peasants was based on the overthrow of established religious, social, and political controls. Luther joined others in calling on the civic authorities to suppress this uprising, which was done at the cost of thousands of lives.

Perhaps this is why Luther asked his contemporaries not to preserve his literary work for future generations, except of course for two documents: the Small Catechism (1529) and a letter to his theological opponent Erasmus. Perhaps he felt that these two teaching documents would not create more instability and contention.

Luther knew that the Reformation had to challenge economic wrongs to bring about the equitable society he dreamed of. He challenged the economic basis of the practice of indulgences, which supported the control of the Catholic Church. He also challenged the fact that banking and the financial world were in the hands of a few.

Our modern world faces similar disruptions to that of Luther's. New technology and outdated, bankrupt political ideas lead us to a situation where children confront world leaders on environmental issues and challenge international corporations to act responsibly. Luther dealt with the multitude of crises and problems at different levels in his own time by being open and contributing to the building of a global community as referred to earlier with respect to his dialogues with people from other regions of the world such as Ethiopia, Constantinople, and England. The response to our present crisis should be informed by his teaching: that we are all members of a global alliance, a rainbow of diversity. We share the environment, the resources, and the wealth of our globe. Our solutions lie not in isolation but in the strength of our community.

Booker T. Washington, one of the first black civil rights activists in the United States, once said, "You can't hold a man down without staying down with him."[4] In the Lutheran understanding of the church as a communion of churches, this observation would be true. The only way developed nations can keep underdeveloped nations in poverty is to stay in poverty with them. No nation can count itself developed when its developmental policies are based on taking advantage of the weaker nations. No nation shall consider itself developed when it leaves others behind.

Luther issues a challenge to us today, a challenge to use wisely and with compassion the wealth that has been granted to us in favor of those who have less. He echoed Saint Paul, who called on the believers to be generous and ready to share their wealth with those in need. We have a responsibility toward the poor, toward refugees, because we were, and may become, poverty-stricken or refugees too, needing the support and care of the global community.

The imagery of the faithful as the salt of the earth is a telling example here. Jesus said, "You are the salt of the earth" (Matt 5:13). But if the salt loses its saltiness, it is of no use to anyone. Salt adds nothing unless it dissolves into the food to give it flavor. Even when we don't see the salt, it can be tasted, and its impact on food is recognized in food preparation. Luther's thoughts and contributions and what he stood for remain to this day, even when they are not apparent. His reformation initiatives opened the church and society for democratic changes that are far reaching. Democratic developments linked to and based on his thoughts are fundamental to making the world a better place, even when the origin of the ethical and democratic standards is not easily identified as being connected to him.

---

4. "You Can't Hold a Man down without Staying down with Him.—Booker T Washington," Thought for the Day, *Tribune*, last modified January 10, 2018, https://tinyurl.com/sunmvbtc.

Lastly, we need to remember that Luther set civil authorities free from the control of Rome, thus starting the slow movement toward modern democracy. It is therefore imperative for congregations, as the most effective operational structures of the church, to challenge the civil authorities to not serve occult powers of finances or of multinational corporations but rather serve the citizens of their countries: the forgotten remnants of the First Nations of our world, the vulnerable members of our societies, the women and children in need of shelter and medical services.

Luther forgotten? Maybe. But his theological and pastoral insights remain resources for the church universal.

STUDY QUESTIONS

1. Why is it important for the church to build relationships across different nationalities, cultures, and religions? What are some of the challenges to building these relationships today?
2. According to Noko, how has Luther continued to shape the work of the church in southern Africa?
3. Noko argues that Luther can help us today address deep problems of wealth inequality. What do you think are some of the problems that need to be addressed? How can or should the church help address these?

3.

Reclaiming the Gospel Legacy
Voices from the Global South

PAUL WEE

GOD LIBERATES IN HISTORY

When Nelson Mandela was released from prison in 1990, one of the first things he did was travel to Geneva, Switzerland, home to international organizations like the United Nations, the World Trade Organization (WTO), and the World Health Organization (WHO). He had spent the last twenty-seven years in prison, eighteen of them on Robben Island, known for its brutal treatment of Black inmates. In one of the most dramatic shifts in modern history, Mandela would go from being the victim of an abusive system of racial oppression to becoming the first president of a free and independent South Africa.

Mandela's Geneva schedule included a visit to the Ecumenical Centre, home to the World Council of Churches (WCC) and the Lutheran World Federation (LWF). I was there as assistant general secretary of the LWF for international affairs and human rights. Mandela had come to express his gratitude for all that the churches had been doing to help secure his freedom and the freedom of the South African people. He would "not be a free man," he claimed, were it not for the work of the churches worldwide. Mandela was referring not to the supportive statements from national churches or the millions of letters received from individual members of the church around the world. He was speaking of the ways in which churches in the Global North had listened to the urgent pleas from South African church leaders. That plea was this: please address the economic and political forces *in your country* that continue to support the oppressive apartheid regime in ours.

Simply to be in the presence of this very humble man was a great honor for me. In my whole being, I felt the deep truth in the confession that "God liberates in history." In and through the myriad of social, economic, and political forces that had converged to create this historic moment, one felt that the Spirit was moving, in the words of Jesus, "to let the oppressed go free" (Luke 4:18).

As I listened to Mandela, I could not help but reflect on how critically important his words were for the church's mission. In essence, he was saying to North American and European churches, "The most helpful role your churches played in our liberation was their efforts to influence the policies of your governments and corporations that supported the *apartheid* status quo economically, politically, and militarily."

The same point was expressed by the bishops of Namibia following the end of the long struggle for freedom in that country that ended on March 21, 1980, the day of Namibian independence. Bishop Kleopas Dumeni of the Evangelical Lutheran Church in Namibia (ELCIN) joined with Anglican and Roman Catholic colleagues in a single expression of gratitude for prayers, advocacy, humanitarian aid, boycotts, protests, and intervention with political leaders by churches and congregations around the world. Is it too much to say that an overwhelming majority of congregations—at least among Lutherans and their partners—in North America was engaged in some way in the cause of freedom for the Namibian people?

Leaders of churches from both countries, South Africa and Namibia, raised the same question: In your discipleship to Jesus Christ, are you willing to go beyond mere charity and address the *causes* of our oppression that are rooted in the policies of your country and ours? Are you willing to get your hands dirty by engaging *systems* that oppress others?

That North American churches and their congregations have the *ability* to do this is not the question here. Congregations are filled with laypeople who not only are passionately committed to justice and equality but have expertise in law, finance, trade, and politics. Congregations in North America have risen to challenges in the past, including participation in struggles for independence itself. Some were part of the antislavery movement. Many are working today with government and police to overcome the shameful legacy of racism. Ability is not the issue here. The question to every congregation is this: In light of the call of Christ, are you *willing*?

Indeed, this was the question put to congregations in the North Atlantic for decades by South African archbishop and Nobel Peace laureate Desmond Tutu.

Following independence, Tutu said, "In South Africa, we could not have achieved our freedom and just peace without the help of people around the world, who through the use of non-violent means, such as boycotts and divestment, encouraged their governments and other corporate actors to reverse decades-long support for the Apartheid regime."[1] Expressing the relevance of the gospel for the *whole* of life characterized the message of a frequent visitor to North America, Archbishop Tutu's colleague Rev. Peter Storey, bishop of the Presbyterian Church of Southern Africa. Storey, who had supervision of the volatile Johannesburg/Soweto area for thirteen years, called for "prophetic evangelism," following Jesus's command to "go into all the world" (Mark 16:15). In one sermon, he urges parishioners to go into the world with "the *whole* gospel, not some amputated portion of it." He says,

> Go into the world of leisure, of economics and politics, human relationships and conflicts, to be agents of transformation, proclaiming "good news to the poor, release for prisoners, recovery of sight for the blind, to let the broken victims go free, . . . and proclaim the year of the Lord's favor."
>
> We must be evangelical enough to know that evil begins in the unredeemed soul, and we must call for conversion; but we must be prophetic enough to know that evil expresses itself most malevolently when it penetrates our corporate life, when we have learned to let our institutions do our sinning for us—so we must work for transformation and justice.[2]

THE CHALLENGE OF THE FORGOTTEN LUTHER

Storey's challenge to the church to recover its evangelical/prophetic vocation by preaching the *whole* gospel captures the essence of our quest to recover the Martin Luther who has been, if not forgotten altogether, then clearly neglected, domesticated, marginalized, limited to the realm of personal piety but essentially removed from the harsh realities of life in the world. As the groundbreaking historical research of Reformation scholar Carter Lindberg has documented, it is the prophetic Luther who has been forgotten, the Luther who was grasped by the gospel's power to drive the church's "work for transformation and justice."

Since our first symposium on this subject took place at the Church of the Reformation in Washington, DC, in November 2015, this underlying thesis has been confirmed over and over again. While some have claimed that Luther's work to transform the structures of the economy and health care and educational systems is "nothing new," many pastors have written to express not only their thanks but also their feelings of surprise and joy: surprise because they found themselves confronting a

---

1. Desmond Tutu, "Divesting from Injustice," *Huffington Post*, June 13, 2010, https://tinyurl.com/2ny9phne.
2. Peter Storey, *With God in the Crucible: Preaching Costly Discipleship* (Nashville: Abingdon, 2002), 152–53.

significant part of the Luther legacy that had not received much attention during seminary studies and joy because they discovered that this
recovered dimension of the Reformation heritage provided such a solid
theological-historical basis for carrying out the type of active, holistic,
gospel-based ministry to which they were committed and in which they
found their deepest satisfaction.

Based on their responses, the participants were surprised to learn how

- Luther's "common chest" economy served to eradicate abject
  poverty in Wittenberg and in the cities and towns of Saxony;

- Luther's Leisnig Order was replicated in cities throughout Saxony and adopted by political leaders in other parts of Germany
  and Europe;

- the Saxony visitation of 1526–28 made Luther aware not only of
  lazy pastors' toothless preaching but also of the depth of poverty
  and the lack of education among clergy and laity;

- Luther's reform of the education system, carried out in con-
  junction with the civil authorities, offered free, state-sponsored
  education for girls, as well as boys;

- the Order of the Common Chest, in underwriting the salaries
  of doctors, became the foundation of universal health care in
  Germany, western Europe, and Scandinavia; and

- Luther's theologically grounded critique of the early profit
  economy shaped a larger popular reaction to the excesses of
  laissez-faire economics in years following.[3]

Critical to all of Luther's reforms that would significantly improve the
quality of life of the common people was their theological grounding
in an understanding of God's free grace in Jesus Christ. This implied
at once a rejection of works righteousness (almsgiving, pilgrimages,
relic collection) as the basis of salvation as well as a rejection of poverty
itself, which followers of Saint Francis of Assisi claimed,[4] as something
pleasing to God. The free gift of grace called for discipleship, for concrete expressions of "faith working through love" (Galatians 5:6), for acts
of charity, and also for critical engagement with the economic forces

3. See Carter Lindberg and Paul Wee, eds., *The Forgotten Luther: Reclaiming the Social-
Economic Dimension of the Reformation* (Minneapolis: Lutheran University Press, 2015); and
Ryan P. Cumming, ed., *The Forgotten Luther II: Reclaiming the Church's Public Witness* (Min-
neapolis: Fortress, 2019). See also Carter Lindberg, "Luther on Wall Street and Welfare,"
Logia 23, no. 4 (Fall 2014): 7–12.
4. Martin Luther, *The Large Catechism*, in *The Book of Concord*, ed. Robert Kolb and
Timothy Wengert (Minneapolis: Fortress, 2000), 418.

and leaders of government. It understood the secular world, with all its hopes and joys—as well as all its misery, oppression, conflict, and pain—as the arena of God's liberating action.

THE COSTLY DIVERSION OF PIETISM

At some point, the Reformation's commitment to the *wholeness* of the gospel proclamation came off the rails. Luther's understanding of God's free grace, embodying as it did not only the salvation of individual souls but the transformation of life in all its dimensions, was replaced by a singular concern for the inner spiritual life of the individual. This took the form of a movement known as Pietism.

The Pietist movement originated within German Lutheranism in the late seventeenth century and then spread to Switzerland, Scandinavia, the Baltic countries, and eventually, North America. Based largely on the theology of Philipp Spener (1635–1705) and August Hermann Francke (1663–1727), it called for an inner spiritual rebirth of individual life, with an emphasis on the discipline of personal devotion, meditation, and a distancing from the concerns of the world.

Pietism continues to exert a strong influence on global Lutheranism. In congregations throughout the world, it shapes the thinking of many parishioners. While some of the strict moralism is gone—for example, no card playing, alcohol use, public discussion of sex, dancing—there remains within Lutheran churches in many countries a lingering suspicion of that part of the church's mission that seeks, however nonpartisan, to shape the life of society through advocacy on legislation and other forms of political action. Even when government fails its pledge to work for the well-being of all, one still hears the call to "keep the church out of politics" altogether.

Yet it must also be noted that not all branches of the Pietist movement advocate noninvolvement in the affairs of the social order. My own grandfather was strongly influenced by lay evangelist Hans Nielsen Hauge (1771–1824), who sought to instill spiritual vitality into what he saw as a cold and lifeless state church of Norway. When my grandfather immigrated to America, he brought with him not only Hauge's disdain for state-sponsored religiosity but also his commitment to the well-being of the common people. He was a member of the school board in Dawson, Minnesota, and took an active role in the affairs of the community.

Generally speaking, however, as a number of writers in this and other Forgotten Luther study books have documented,[5] the role of Pietism has tended to emphasize the personal dimension of Christian life at the expense

---

5. See Carter Lindberg's chapter in this volume.

of a Christian's involvement in the public arena. It has kept the central evangelical tenet of *justification by faith* (Augsburg Confession, article 5) in the virtual prison of individualism without drawing its connection to justice in society. As Tim Huffman stated so forcefully in his chapter in the first *Forgotten Luther* volume, "Luther: Forgotten, but Not Gone," in speaking of a 1984 meeting of theologians from the North and the South, "[We] agreed that justification is fundamentally making justice or working for justice, and that Lutherans had sometimes gotten justification right but then tended to miss the critical and inescapable move from justification to a commitment to work for justice."[6] Perhaps the most devastating consequence of what might be termed a *doctrinal disconnect* was the effect of Pietism in its German birthplace during the rise of National Socialism in the 1930s. One of the more disastrous implications of the call to "keep the church out of politics" was the church's acquiescence—even *complicity*—in the face of the rise of the ideology of Aryan supremacy, totalitarianism, Nazi aggression, and the systematic murder of six million Jews. In light of this, and in the face of even more recent attempts to identify political agendas with God's will, the fact that some church people continue to advocate for silence or noninvolvement in the public arena is troubling.

Pietism had an especially strong influence on the missionary movement in the nineteenth and twentieth centuries. Although this is not the occasion to document this long and complex history, it needs to be noted that some missionaries who came to Africa, Asia, and Latin America from Scandinavia, North America, and Europe were strongly influenced by Pietism. Generally speaking, this meant that the churches under their care were counseled to avoid involvement in the political-economic systems of their respective countries.

This in no way implies, however, that the missionaries were not committed to the total well-being of the people they came to serve. On the contrary, they built hospitals and schools, taught and translated, oversaw the construction of irrigation and sanitation systems, drilled for sources of clean water, and developed systems for medical diagnosis in remote villages. This is a heritage of healing and hope that the church can be proud of, even as we today recognize the shortcomings of early models of international mission. I personally know—or know about—dozens of committed individuals who set out in faith to foreign lands, who sacrificed lives of relative luxury and braved disease and discomfort, and whose children coped with boarding schools, distant travel, uncertainty, physical and mental health challenges, and discrimination. For some, a return to

---

6. Tim Huffman, "Luther: Forgotten, but Not Gone," in Lindberg and Wee, *Forgotten Luther*, 73.

home was difficult because of a lack of adequate health care, financial limitations, or the absence of a North American community that is even remotely able to comprehend what they had experienced. The church owes these people a great deal of gratitude.

In addition, their work has been highly productive. Because of their efforts in the training of Indigenous leaders and helping form self-reliant churches, one might say that they have brought the missionary movement full circle. Churches that were once struggling simply to survive have become strong and thriving communities of faith for millions of people. As congregations in North America and Western Europe are well aware, churches in the Global South have in turn been sending their own homegrown missionaries to the North for decades.

As Dr. David Vickner, former director of the Global Mission unit of the former Lutheran Church in America (LCA), frequently noted, the relationship between churches in the South and the North continues to mature, "from dependence to independence to interdependence." This realization of genuine interdependence, or mutuality, remains a pillar of global mission today. It acknowledges the fact that all churches, regardless of economic status or geography, have gifts of the Spirit to share with each other.

A MODEL OF MUTUALITY IN GLOBAL MISSION

This mutuality is embodied most tangibly today in the mission policy and leadership of the executive director of the Global Mission unit of the Evangelical Lutheran Church in America (ELCA), Rafael Malpica Padilla. Born and reared in Puerto Rico, Malpica Padilla has been a pioneer in the development of a model of mission based on genuine mutuality in which church leaders, lay and clergy, are called to listen to, share with, and accompany one another in pursuing a common goal. Following in the footsteps of his predecessors, including a number of those to whom this study book is dedicated—Bo Sorenson, Mark Thomsen, and Bonnie Jensen—Malpica Padilla has shaped an ELCA companion synod program in which participants have learned what it means not only to give but to receive, not only to speak but to listen, not only to teach but to be taught by churches of the Global South. Furthermore, the program Young Adults in Global Mission (YAGM), discussed in more detail in Malpica Padilla's chapter in this book, has exposed young people to challenging situations abroad that have forced them to think outside the box with respect to designing creative solutions to problems. Perhaps even more important, these young people, together with counterparts from the Global South, have put together models of mission that involve intense collaboration.

In light of such a positive development, how can it be justifiably maintained that the Pietist movement had a negative effect on the growth of churches in the Global South? The fact remains that in spite of growing maturity, self-reliance, and interdependence, many churches in the Global South had to discover on their own the biblical-theological legitimacy for addressing demonic ideologies and systems of political and economic and racial oppression. In Africa, a major factor in the formation of a theology to address these realities, including a biblical justification for carrying out active resistance against them, had its deepest source in the awareness that *all* of life was bound together in a single interrelated whole. This meant a rejection of the dualistic thinking prevalent in Pietism that drew a sharp line between the spiritual and the material, the soul and the body, the church and the world. Religion was not one area of life that could be, either academically or practically, separated from other areas, such as the political or the social. It was rather the integrating factor for all of life. As Kenyan John Mbiti famously noted, to be African is to be religious.[7]

One who felt the powerful influence of this uniquely African sense of the wholeness of life was the late South African Lutheran theologian Dr. Manas Buthelezi. Convinced that religion was integrated into every aspect of daily life, he struggled against what he considered to be the restricting influence of the Pietist missionaries from Europe and North America. He wrote, "It's a well-known fact that when Christianity was brought to Africa this wholeness of life was disrupted. This is mainly because the brand of Christianity that was introduced was heavily influenced by Pietism. Pietism paved the way for a total secularization of the natural, namely the spheres of work, politics, economics and as a matter of fact all that gave concrete meaning to daily life. It set the inner life rather than the social as the place where God and man may enter into relationship with each other."[8]

Converging with the reaction to Pietism by church leaders in the Global South was the sheer weight of the oppressive governmental forces that were taking such a huge toll on communities, whether these were the heavily militarized *apartheid* countries of Namibia, Rhodesia, and South Africa or the brutal dictatorships of Guatemala, Brazil, or Argentina. People were rising up against these forces, and the churches simply had to make it known which side they were on. And that choice, whether openly stated or not, presupposed a prior (theological) decision on the proper role of the church in the political and economic realms.

---

7. John Mbiti, *Introduction to African Religions*, 2nd ed. (Oxford: Heinemann, 1991), 108.

8. Quoted by Rev. Gudina Tumsa in Gudina Tumsa, "Serving the Whole Man," in *Witness and Discipleship: Leadership of the Church in Multi-ethnic Ethiopia in a Time of Revolution: The Essential Writings of Gudina Tumsa, General Secretary of the Ethiopian Evangelical Church Mekane Yesus (1929–1979)* (Addis Ababa, Ethiopia: Gudina Tumsa Foundation, 2003), 119.

IN THE SPIRIT OF THE FORGOTTEN
LUTHER: THE CASE OF GUATEMALA

In this final section, I would like to test the assumptions expressed earlier with concrete reference to one country of the Global South, Guatemala. It represents, to my thinking, a primary contemporary example of how the principles that Luther employed in forming a faith-based response to a crisis in his day have relevance for our response to a crisis in our own day. Luther's situation is far from ours of course, but some of the principles that guided his thinking remain highly relevant today.

I have selected the case of Guatemala because it represents so realistically an example of Christian mission in which

- genuine mutuality begins with listening to the cries of the people,
- concern for the salvation of the individual includes commitment to the well-being of the community,
- acts of charity lead to the establishing of conditions for justice through a new order on the ground, and
- addressing economic inequality demands interaction with civil authorities.

In brief, the example of Guatemala represents a striking example of community transformation in the spirit of the forgotten Luther. It also expresses a model of mission in which an initiative from churches in the Global South found a response from churches in the North, resulting in collaboration with a common goal. Time and space permit only a brief overview here.

Historical Overview

The violent suppression of the Mayan population in Guatemala was not limited to the period commonly known as La Violencia (1978–84), years that witnessed the scorched-earth campaign of military presidents Romeo Lucas Garcia and Efrain Rios Montt. On the contrary, the violence extends back 450 years to the Spanish conquest, when brutal colonialism and a religious drive to "convert the heathen Indians" served to nearly destroy traditional Mayan culture and religion. The conquest signaled the beginning of a long period of genocide, exploitation, and enslavement.

In a general sense, one can say that five centuries of Guatemalan and Central American history have been the history of conflict between two civilizations, one being an Indigenous civilization expressed in Mayan, Incan, and Aztec culture and the other a European civilization characterized by expansionist dreams, economic domination, and an exaggerated sense of its own virtue. The European—in this case, Spanish—civilization involved control by the political military, the landowners, and the church.

Mention needs to be made of one critical moment in the modern period of Guatemalan history. On June 27, 1954, the Central Intelligence Agency (CIA) of the United States engineered an invasion of Guatemala and overthrew the democratically elected government of President Jacobo Arbenz Guzman. The rationale for the invasion had to do not simply with the socialist leanings of Arbenz or his support of labor unions and land reform but with his expropriation of uncultivated lands claimed by the US-based banana interest, the United Fruit Company of Boston. President Arbenz was replaced with the autocratic, repressive government of Carlos Castillo Armas, who immediately put a halt to labor unions and to a land reform perceived to be a threat to the banana industry. Reforms designed to overcome the vast discrepancies between the wealthy few and the millions of rural poor were terminated. The Armas regime became the first in a series of brutal military governments that perpetuated a legacy of domination and exploitation not unlike that of the conquistadores five centuries earlier.

Guatemalan theologian and "poet of the Guatemalan genocide" Julia Esquivel (1930–2019) recalls life in the coup's aftermath in her poem "They Have Threatened Us With Resurrection." She wrote,

> What keeps us from sleeping
> is that they have threatened us with Resurrection!
> Because every evening
> though weary of killings,
> an endless inventory since 1954,
> yet we go on loving life
> and do not accept their death![9]

The suppression of democracy in Guatemala since 1954 contributed to the formation of various political opposition groups, many of whose members were initially hunted down and killed. With the breakdown of peaceful efforts for change, the armed conflict began in earnest in 1960. It was inspired by Castro's revolution a year earlier and was supported both ideologically and materially by the Soviet Union. In the early 1980s, four of these opposition groups banded together to form a single umbrella resistance group, the Guatemalan National Revolutionary Unity (URNG).

9. Julia Esquivel, "They Have Threatened Us With Resurrection," *Spiritus: A Journal of Christian Spirituality* 3, no. 1 (Spring 2003): 96–101.

Vatican II

Then something quite historic took place. Looking innocent enough, it was called the Second Vatican Council, gathering prelates of the global Roman Catholic Church in Rome for deliberations from 1962 through 1965. Called into being by Pope John XXIII, Vatican II, as it came to be known, was nothing short of revolutionary, giving shape to the theology and mission of the Roman Catholic Church. Calling on congregations not only to be committed to the poor but to actually *be* poor for the sake of the poor was nothing short of transforming, especially in Latin America. Vatican II said something even more radical—namely, that human sin was to be found not only in the individual souls of people but in the structures and practices of political and economic life.

Such affirmations inspired a theology of liberation not only among Roman Catholic theologians but also among Lutherans, Presbyterians, Methodists, Anglicans, Moravians, and Baptists. Vatican II inspired church leaders in Central America and Latin America to invest more authority in the laity of the church, in women, and in base communities dedicated to worship, prayer, and common action on behalf of the poorest members of society. It said this to oppressed people: God has created you with dignity and for freedom; now *be* what God has called you to be.

In the years following, the Roman Catholic bishops' conferences in Medellín (1968) and Puebla (1979) interpreted the meaning of Vatican II for the people of Latin America. This meant that a portion of the church leadership would become much more critical of oppressive, authoritarian governments. Lay catechists of the Roman Catholic Church who took up the challenge of the church to identify with the aspirations of the poor and sought to alter unjust structures that oppressed the poor were tortured and killed by the hundreds in Guatemala and throughout Central America.

The Bible itself became a dangerous book. There were to be many martyrs, including Roman Catholic archbishop Oscar Romero; Catholic priest Rutilio Grande; Baptist lay leader Maria Gomez; Lutheran pastor David Fernandez; Roman Catholic sisters Ita Ford, Maura Clarke, and Dorothy Kazel; and laywoman Jean Donovan from the United States. On October 7, 1989, Lutheran pastor Phil Anderson and I met with Fr. Ignacio Ellacuría and his colleagues at the José Simeón Cañas Central American University (UCA) in San Salvador just weeks before they were tortured and killed by the Salvadoran military.

No Peace without Justice: The Role of the LWF

It is important to mention Vatican II because it was an integral part of the deep background that made possible a peace agreement in Guatemala, brokered in large part by the LWF. In brief, this is what happened.

Thanks to the intervention of the then pope John Paul II and his papal nuncio in Guatemala, LWF Latin America representative Phil Anderson and I were given the opportunity to meet with the minister of defense, Hector Gramajo, and members of the high command of the Guatemalan military. Would the military and the government be willing to send a delegation to engage in "quiet talks" with the URNG outside the country? We offered a secure meeting place and would meet under the banner of the National Reconciliation Commission, a structure set up in accordance with a framework (Esquipulas II) that had been developed by Costa Rican president Oscar Arias Sanchez. After deliberation, the minister of defense agreed. For its part, the Political Diplomatic Commission of the URNG also accepted the invitation. With security provided by the government of Norway, we would meet during the last week of March 1990.

Held in a chalet in the Holmenkollen mountains outside of Oslo, the occasionally volatile meeting produced, on the final day, an agreement that would eventually bring an end to thirty-six years of armed conflict that claimed the lives of more than two hundred thousand. But it would take six more years of intense negotiations to bring deep changes in the economy, the structure of political representation, the role of business and trade, and the role of the private sector. It is not an oversimplification to say that where the government wanted only an end to hostilities, the opposition URNG and the nongovernmental sector, including the churches, demanded deep changes in an unjust economic and political system.

As the negotiations continued following the Oslo meeting, the parties were invited to Washington, DC, by the US government. One day during the visit, the participants took part in a service of dedication to peace at the Church of the Reformation on Capitol Hill. The large sanctuary was filled, with the opposing delegations (wisely) seated on each side of the center aisle. Rigoberta Menchú Tum, the future Nobel Peace Prize winner, had difficulty deciding on which side of the aisle she would sit. But it was a scene to be remembered—US political leaders participating with leaders of the guerilla URNG and members of the Guatemalan government and military in a service of prayer for a just and lasting peace in Guatemala.

Although neither side got everything it wanted, a final peace agreement was ceremoniously signed in the presence of the UN secretary-general Boutros Boutros-Ghali, Guatemalan president Alvaro Arzu, members of the Guatemalan government and military, the four commanders of the URNG, and the UN negotiator Jean Arnault, whose expertise was critical during the years of final negotiation and during the phase of demilitarization and disarmament. There were representatives of several countries, including the "country friends" (Paises Amigos) that had played such an important role in the final years of the peace process: Spain, Norway, Venezuela, Mexico, and in the later stages, the United States. Present also were leaders of the WCC, the Latin America Council of Churches (CLAI), and the National Council of the Churches of Christ in the USA (NCCCUSA).

The presiding bishop of the Roman Catholic Church in Guatemala invited all of the Christian faith communities to participate in a service of thanksgiving in the Cathedral Metropolitan Basilica of Santiago de Guatemala. Among those who read from Scripture and prayed was Vitallino Similox, an Indigenous Mayan leader who was president of the Presbyterian Church of Guatemala. It was Similox who had pleaded continually with churches in the United States to intercede with their government to cease providing military hardware to the Guatemalan regime. He confided his joy over the fact that churches in the North had listened.

In the days following the signing, Julia Esquivel would say this: "I make reference to the Lutheran World Federation, which was determinative and about which little has been said. It was the Lutheran World Federation that pushed, motivated and stimulated until the dialogue between the guerrillas, the government and the army finally came together into negotiations for peace."[10] Throughout the process, among the participating churches from the North and the South, there was a single overarching principle that served as a guide: *peace is not simply the absence of conflict; it is the presence of justice.* And not simply justice as adherence to a set of legal requisites, but justice understood biblically, which is to say, holistically. Justice, as theologians of liberation from the North and the South agree, is the presence of *shalom*—that is, a condition of holistic balance in which the gifts of God's creation are shared with equity, where no one has too much and no one too little, where no one is oppressing and no one is being oppressed.

One voice from the Global South that expresses this most powerfully today is that of the Argentine pope Francis. Since becoming the leader of the Roman Catholic Church, Pope Francis has been working continuously on efforts to bring about this sense of *shalom* through specific structural changes in both church and society. On November 24, 2013, the Sunday

---

10. Quoted in Rudy Nelson and Shirley Nelson, prod., *Precarious Peace: God and Guatemala*, narrated by Martin Marty (Worcester, PA: Gateway Films, Vision Video, 1993): https://vimeo.com/ondemand/precariouspeace.

of Christ the King, Pope Francis issued an apostolic exhortation entitled *Evangelii gaudium (The Joy of the Gospel)*. Clearly troubled by the widening gap between rich and poor, the pope addressed an issue that preoccupied Luther and continues to challenge the church—namely, bringing the message of Christ to bear on the economic life. He says,

> The need to resolve the structural causes of poverty cannot be delayed, not only for the pragmatic reason of its urgency for the good order of society, but because society needs to be cured of a sickness which is weakening and frustrating it, and which can only lead to new crises. Welfare projects, which meet certain urgent needs, should be considered merely temporary responses. As long as the problems of the poor are not radically resolved by rejecting the absolute autonomy of markets and financial speculation and by attacking the structural causes of inequality, no solution will be found for the world's problems or, for that matter, to any problems. Inequality is the root of social ills.[11]

Here Martin Luther and Pope Francis would be of the same mind.

A Postscript on Guatemala

The good news is that the long and destructive war is over. Yet that country is unfortunately far from being the model of justice and peace for which the people have longed and for which so many have given their lives. Gang terror has replaced that of the military, the poor continue to die for lack of nutrition, and the wealthy still live in fortified enclaves protected by watchdogs and armed guards. Some good friends committed to working for equity have died, among them my colleague Phil Anderson, a Lutheran pastor who listened to the cries of the people and who in turn earned their respect and their trust. In the face of the deaths of so many who were part of the struggle in Central America, it is possible to become resigned, even despairing.

At the same time, reflecting on their sacrifice—and let us add to theirs the sacrifice of missionaries who over the years set out in faith to proclaim the good news of Jesus Christ and to improve the quality of life of the poor—one cannot help but be encouraged and renewed for the task.

In his day, Martin Luther undertook a visitation to the towns and rural areas to the south of Wittenberg during the years 1526–28 at the suggestion of Elector John the Steadfast of Saxony. For Luther, the visitation reflected the practice of Jesus as well as that of Saint Paul, who, at one point, said to Barnabas, "Come, let us return and visit the believers in every city

---

11. Pope Francis, *Evangelii gaudium* (Vatican City: Vatican, 2013), sec. 202, https://tinyurl.com/cect98hd.

where we proclaimed the word of the Lord and see how they are doing" (Acts 15:36). During his visits in Saxony, Luther listened to townspeople and farmers, to artisans and housewives, to merchants and preachers. He also listened to the children, to the girls as well as the boys. Out of that visitation came the Small Catechism and the Large Catechism, both in 1529. Less well known perhaps, there also emerged a deeper commitment on Luther's part to continue his work with the political authorities to alter the structures that condemned people to lives of poverty, illiteracy, and poor health. The visitation, which resulted in extensive reforms to the new church, brought immense hope as well to the daily lives of the common people.

Despite disappointments, the work of churches from the North and the South to bring change to the lives of the poor in Guatemala was, like Luther's experience in Saxony, filled with immense encouragement and hope. We need only be open to God's word speaking to us from others who are walking with us on the way and remember the admonition of Saint Paul: "So let us not grow weary in doing what is right, for we will reap at harvest time, if we do not give up" (Gal 6:9).

STUDY QUESTIONS

1. How does Wee challenge Lutherans, especially North American Lutherans, to think differently about Luther and faith?
2. Do you think that Wee is right that Luther's theology has been forgotten or domesticated? What might be the consequences of this for the church?
3. What might Luther say about our world today? What might be in his Ninety-Five Theses if they were written this year?
4. What might a common chest look like today? What sorts of social programs might be needed to support it?

4.

"And Though This World with Devils Filled"

Reshaping the World in Hope

MITRI RAHEB

When it was clear that I wanted to study theology after feeling a call to ministry, everyone suggested that I go to Germany. Germany, the land of Luther and the land of the Reformation, was perceived as the best place for me to study Lutheran theology at its origins. Lutheran theological thought at Marburg, Germany, was a very sophisticated but theoretical theology.[1] It seems to me that Lutheran theology in the course of five centuries was domesticated and had lost its teeth.[2] It was the context in Palestine that opened for me a new window to understanding the socio-political dimension of Luther's theology. It was the context of occupation that helped me rediscover Luther in a new way and do ministry with a different scope and dimension.

I returned from Germany in May 1987, and six months later, the first intifada (Palestinian uprising)[3] began. I saw our people rising to resist Israeli occupation and oppression. I saw Palestinian children facing the Israeli military tanks with stones in their hands, like David when he was facing Goliath (1 Sam 17). Such clashes were taking place almost daily around our sanctuary. Several times while preaching from the pulpit I had to stop because the shooting by the Israeli soldiers just outside the door to the sanctuary was so loud that it made our members grip their pews. Several church elders were imprisoned without trial or charges on so-called administrative detention. Several members from the youth group were jailed because of their political activity.

---

1. As an example, see Gerhard Ebeling, *Luther* (Tübingen, Germany: J. C. B. Mohr, 1984).
2. New approaches to Lutheran theology were initiated by Ulrich Duchrow in Germany in five volumes: Ulrich Duchrow, ed., *Radicalizing Reformation*, 5 vols. (Berlin: LIT, 2015–16).
3. Mitri Raheb, *I Am a Palestinian Christian* (Minneapolis: Fortress, 1994).

I felt like I was being thrown into cold water with only two choices: swim or sink.

It wasn't only that I was a fresh graduate who had little experience and was new to this emerging reality, but it was the question whether the gospel of Jesus Christ has anything to say in a context like this and whether the Lutheran theology of the four "solas" had a sociopolitical dimension.

If theology is to be relevant to the socioeconomic and sociopolitical life of the people, we must start with the people. Luther spoke of the importance of listening to the ordinary people (house mothers, children on the streets, and the ordinary men at the market).[4] The more I started listening to the people, and the more I confronted these questions with the Bible, the more I started discovering that our Christian faith and our Lutheran heritage have sociopolitical dimensions that have been diluted with time.

In this essay, I will focus on three dimensions of the "solas": sola Scriptura (Scripture alone), sola gratia (grace alone), and sola spes (hope alone).

SOLA SCRIPTURA

In 1988, George, a young Lutheran boy and an active member of our youth group, was jailed without trial and sent to prison in one of the harshest and largest Israeli jails in the Negev desert, known as Ktzi'ot, or Ansar III. Palestinian prisoners were housed in tents in the middle of the desert, where the days are very hot and the nights are cold enough to get into one's bones. At times, there were over six thousand Palestinian prisoners there, making it the largest prison in the world. During the first intifada, it was estimated that 2 percent of all Palestinian males over sixteen years old were jailed in that prison.[5] I was not allowed to visit George, but George used to send our youth group letters from his prison. Prisoners were writing their letters on the thin cigarette paper, yet it was still forbidden to get letters out of the prison. We were very worried about George; we knew of the different torture methods that Israelis were using in their prisons. We were worried about his physical, psychological, and spiritual well-being.

The youth group was very anxious when they received the first letter from George. We were surprised that the letter showed signs not of despair, fear, or hate but rather of encouragement and hope. He was encouraging us not to get weary in our meetings. Then we got the second letter. We

---

4. "Man muss die Mutter im Hause, die Kinder auf den Gassen, den gemeinen Mann auf dem Markt fragen und denselbigen aufs Maul sehen, wie sie reden und danach dolmetschen, so versten sie es dann und merken, dass man Deutsch mit ihnen redet."

5. *Prison Conditions in Israel and the Occupied Territories: A Middle East Watch Report* (New York: Human Rights Watch, 1991), 18, 64, https://www.hrw.org/reports/Israel914.pdf.

were amazed that George was writing about the role of women in society and how important it is that women are fully engaged in the society and in the struggle.

These letters became an eye-opener for us. Suddenly, we understood how we must approach the biblical texts. Most of the biblical texts were written in the context of occupation: Assyrian, Babylonian, Persian, Greek, or Roman. Many of the Prophetic texts were drafted in exile; many of Paul's letters, like George's, were written in prison. Many texts were underground texts and had to be written in a secret style known as "apocalyptic." This is the actual *Sitz im Leben* of the texts.

Luther's texts were in no way different. Luther's translation of the Bible was done underground. His life was under constant threat. Luther was facing not only the pope and the kaiser of his time, and thus the whole empire, but like Paul, he felt he was up against the devil himself. In this context, he wrote his very famous Reformation song. The third stanza of "A Mighty Fortress Is Our God" reads, "And though this world with devils filled."[6] We can't read Luther away from his biography and his own context of struggle. His words, works, and life belong closely together. His words lose their teeth if they become theoretical dogmas rather than powerful proclamations for real-life situations.

When Luther declared his sola Scriptura, he wanted to give people direct access to the Scripture without having to go through the narrow gate of church tradition. Sola Scriptura thus did not mean in any way a fundamentalist reading of the Bible, but it meant to release the Bible from church captivity so that one can have a fresh look at it and discover its liberating power. For Luther, it was clear that church tradition had spiritualized the Bible in such a way that it had lost its relevance and liberating power. To bypass the monopoly tradition of spiritualizing the Bible through the church, Luther was eager to give attention to the literal aspect of the text.[7] This literal understanding should not be confused with literalism; rather, it's a way to save the worldly relevance of the text. The biblical texts are real, written in a real time and place and drafted in a context of struggle and oppression. Such a "literal" understanding of the writings leads us to discover them as texts of resistance rather than texts of compliance, texts of struggle rather than texts of submission.

As Palestinian Christians, we can relate very much to the context of Jesus, Paul, and Luther. Like Jesus, who lived under Roman occupation,

---

6. Martin Luther, "A Mighty Fortress Is Our God," in Committee on Christian Education, *Trinity Hymnal* (Suwanee, GA: Great Commission, 1961), hymn 81, https://opc.org/books/TH-orig.pdf.

7. Martin Luther, "Answer to the Hyperchristian, Hyperspiritual, and Hyperlearned Book by Goat Emser in Leipzig—Including Some Thoughts regarding His Companion, the Fool Murner," 1521, in *LW* 39:178.

we have been living under Israeli occupation for too long. Like Paul, we feel that our struggle is not against "flesh and blood, but against principalities . . . of this world" (Eph 6:12 KJV)—in our case, against a strong and well-funded Israeli lobby. And, like Luther, we feel that we are facing an empire that is backing the Israeli military as well as Christian Zionist groups who are backing the occupation theologically.[8]

The church has unfortunately domesticated the biblical texts. Liberation became salvation. Lutheran theology was domesticated too. Many Lutheran theologians were preaching justification without justice: a white, middle-class, affluent theology that is foreign from its original context. Anglo-Saxon white theology transformed these texts of liberation to become texts that support occupation. People in the Global South were taught about the freedom of the "Christian Menschen,"[9] but this freedom had little relevance to the freedom of their communities. The church was entrusted with saving the souls of the Indigenous people while the empire went on to strip them of their land and resources. The texts of liberation became texts of colonization. This was the case not only in North[10] and South America,[11] Africa,[12] and Australia[13] but also in Palestine.[14]

The context of the first intifada opened our eyes to read the Bible in a fresh way, away from the European theological lens that has blurred it. The biblical texts are highly political in their own nature. If we take sola Scriptura seriously, there is no way to be neutral or apolitical. The sola Scriptura properly understood can help us rediscover the revolutionary and, thus, liberating power of the Scriptures.

SOLA GRATIA

Like sola Scriptura, sola gratia was domesticated in the course of history as well. It became the recipe for individual salvation. However, sola gratia was proclaimed originally in a context where religion was exercising socioeconomic pressure on the whole community. Religion was structured

---

8. Christian Zionism (website), accessed March 23, 2021, http://www.christianzionism.org.

9. *WA* 7:20–38.

10. George E. Tinker, *Missionary Conquest: The Gospel and Native American Cultural Genocide* (Minneapolis: Fortress Press, 1993); Steven Salaita, *Inter/Nationalism: Decolonizing Native America and Palestine*, Indigenous Americas (Minneapolis: University of Minnesota Press, 2016).

11. Walter Altmann, *Luther and Liberation: A Latin American Perspective*, 2nd ed. (Minneapolis: Fortress, 2016).

12. Michael Prior, *The Bible and Colonialism: A Moral Critique* (Sheffield, UK: Sheffield Academic, 1997).

13. Norman C. Habel, *Acknowledgement of the Land and Faith of Aboriginal Custodians after following the Abraham Trail* (Eugene, OR: Wipf & Stock, 2018).

14. Steven Salaita, *The Holy Land in Transit: Colonialism and the Quest for Canaan*, Middle East Studies beyond Dominant Paradigms (Syracuse, NY: Syracuse University Press, 2006).

in such a way as to keep people hostage to fear (from God), captives to religious practices that were not for "free" and where salvation was offered for a fee. The problem, therefore, was not so much a mere theological one but a systemic one too. The church in that context was exercising a kind of religious terror. This systemic dimension was overlooked.

Often in situations of political or economic oppression, people tend to resort to religion. Religion becomes an important element of people's identity. Confronted with a mighty and unjust reality, people start longing for the justice that only God can bring. Yet for God to bring about justice, people need first to adhere to God's laws. People in such contexts can become obsessed with spreading the law, creating additional laws, and competing to fulfill every iota of its tenants.

Slowly, religious groups and institutions try to take over public life, to dictate how to dress, how often to pray, and how to behave in public as well as in private. Slowly and without much noise, they penetrate one social arena after the other. Once religious movements gain enough clout, they do not hesitate to assume power, to pronounce death penalties over individuals who oppose their thinking, and to eliminate anyone who dares to question their religious standing. Over time, religion becomes the basis to assume more economic power. A whole economic system builds around religious institutions. And yet these religious laws become themselves oppressive toward their own people. Jesus understood this like no other when he stated, "They tie up heavy burdens, hard to bear, and lay them on the shoulders of others" (Matt 23:4).

Jesus was sentenced to death not under Roman law alone but in the name of divine law too. It was a unique combination of state terror coupled with religious terror that brought Jesus to the cross. Jesus was sentenced to death because he was seen as blasphemous. He was accused of breaking the religious laws, of daring to question the religious practices of his time, and of challenging the religious authorities. Those who killed him believed they were doing God a favor. The Gospel of John refers to this exact phenomenon when it says, "An hour is coming when those who kill you will think that by doing so they are offering worship to God" (John 16:2). We must see the execution of Jesus on the cross in this context.[15]

This was the context of Luther. Luther was excommunicated by the religious institution of his time because his sola gratia not only was about individual salvation but questioned the whole religious system that was in place. Luther was fortunate to escape the execution. Other reformers had to pay with their lives. To understand Luther correctly, we need to connect his teaching with his biography and his larger context.

---

15. Mitri Raheb and Suzanne Watts Henderson, *The Cross in Contexts: Suffering and Redemption in Palestine* (Maryknoll, NY: Orbis, 2017).

For the peoples of the Middle East, surrounded by an influx of conservative religious movements and parties, all of whom claim to be orthodox, the sola gratia is very important. Sola gratia in this context is not so much about individual salvation, something still propagated by free church groups funded by American Christians, but about a society free from social pressures and religious control of the public sphere, where women and minorities are often the ones paying the price. Sola gratia is thus a call for liberation—liberation from oppressive social systems imposed by religious institutions. Sola gratia is a revolutionary call to dismantle oppressive socioreligious structures.

What role can Christians play today in preventing religious structures from controlling the public sphere? What role can Christians play in the Middle Eastern context, where Islam is the dominant religion? To reflect on this question, Dar al-Kalima University College of Arts and Culture initiated the Christian Academic Forum for Citizenship in the Arab World (CAFCAW). To that end, in 2011, we gathered a group of Christian intellectuals from six countries: Palestine, Egypt, Lebanon, Syria, Jordan, and Iraq. The authors came from a variety of faith traditions, including Coptic, Maronite, Orthodox, Lutheran, Baptist, and Muslim intellectuals. This process led to the drafting of a document entitled *From the Nile to the Euphrates: The Call of Faith and Citizenship*.[16] This ecumenical document was publically launched on December 6, 2014, in Beirut.

What distinguishes this document is its focus on the notion of citizenship. The role of the state is to safeguard the rights of all its citizens. On the other hand, religion has an important role to inspire its followers to undertake "full and responsible citizenship."[17] The document calls for a "conscientious and dynamic faith" that does not run away or hide from the challenges of society but instead engages society for the good of its citizens.[18] A theology of grace can be part of the solution, while religious fanaticism constitutes part of the problem. The alternative to state and religious terror is a society based on civil laws, freedom, and equal citizenship irrespective of one's religious convictions, cultural identity, socioeconomic status, or race. Sola gratia thus liberates Christians to perceive and to work toward a graceful community away from state or religious terror.

In the words of the founding members of the CAFCAW, we read,

> We believe in Jesus Christ, the incarnate Word of God, who dwelt among us, who taught, healed and went about doing good, calling all peoples to repentance and righteousness, and proclaiming liberty and goodness. Therefore,

16. The Christian Academic Forum for Citizenship in the Arab World (CAFCAW), *From the Nile to the Euphrates: The Call of Faith and Citizenship* (Bethlehem: Diyar, 2014).
17. CAFCAW, 5.
18. CAFCAW, 5.

we are committed to following his path, and to continuing his mission in the service of humanity through the ministries of education, healing, development, culture and the arts. We do this as we also pursue justice, seek and make peace, and advocate human rights in our Arab context. We believe in Jesus Christ who died on the cross and in the victory of his resurrection. He experienced the agony and hardships of human life, endured humiliation, and suffered the pain of injustice and persecution. He then rose triumphantly, proclaiming the dawn of a new era. Therefore, we are committed to solidarity with those who are crushed, weakened, and oppressed. We shall not give in to despair or to the logic of death, but will live with the power and hope of the resurrection, and in our conduct shall bear witness to the sanctity of life. . . . We believe in eternal life, and realize that people in our region believe in life after death, but are starting to despair of the possibility of life with dignity before death. Therefore, we are committed to strive toward ensuring a decent life for people in our time and place. As we live through these difficult times in the history of our region, when Christians are suffering from persecution, demonization, and forced displacement, we realize that this calamity does not target just Christians, but the country as a whole. This is our understanding and declaration of a conscientious and active faith, positive involvement, and active participation. Therefore . . . we believe and commit.[19]

SOLA SPES

One of the words that is underrepresented in the writing on Luther is the word *hope*. In the solas, we miss *sola spes*, although hope played an important role in Luther's thinking. In fact, he described it as the "sum of all Christian teaching."[20]

He wrote on hope when dealing with Psalm 5 already in 1516–17.[21] In Luther's thinking, hope has nothing to do with optimism. Optimism derives from optimum: the best that is to come, the best that ultimately will come. For Luther, this would have meant hoping in one's own merit. But merit leads ultimately to despair. In this commentary, Luther describes the Christian as "sinner in reality" yet "saint in hope."[22]

Later, hope was strongly connected to Luther's personal struggle. Luther faced immense challenges in his life—persecution, adversaries, and death—and was often pushed to the brink of despair. He often felt as "though this world with devils filled." Such a state of anguish, says Luther, pushes the faithful to stop believing in one's own abilities, merit, and strength and to put all hope in Christ, the crucified.

19. CAFCAW, 4.
20. Kurt Aland, ed., *Lutherlexikon*, 4th ed. (Göttingen, Germany: Vandenhoeck and Ruprecht, 1989), 181.
21. Martin Luther, *Evangelium und leben*, ed. Horst Beintker (Berlin: Evangelische Verlagsanstalt, 1983), 20–31.
22. Luther, 25.

Yet putting one's hope in God doesn't mean sitting down and waiting for salvation to come riding in on a white horse. Christian hope is often described by a saying that is attributed to Luther, though scholars doubt today if it was really from him, that says, "Even if I knew that the world was coming to an end tomorrow, I would go out today into the garden and plant an apple tree." In this sense, hope is not a positive outlook on history, the idea that tomorrow is going to be better or that the Lord will find a way. Rather, hope is what we do today even though the world might come to an end tomorrow.

It is a call to action today despite the grim outlook. What is important here, though, is that this action is not a reaction. A reaction would be to try to secure oneself, or to escape into a church to pray, or to meet to celebrate the countdown. Planting an apple tree is also not something that will turn the world upside down, not something that will change the course of history. It is doing the ordinary, yet it is the context that makes it extraordinary. Planting a tree in a context like this might seem crazy. It doesn't make sense: a long-term investment when time is running out. However, what is crucial is that the planting is done in the garden, in the society, in the public space. The church is called to break outside its own walls.

At Christmas Lutheran Church in Bethlehem in the early 1990s, during the first intifada when the clashes were taking place around our church, we opened a church guesthouse. We felt obliged to invite church groups from around the globe to "come and see." At that moment, it seemed like a crazy thing to do. Tourism was at a decade low. Groups stopped coming to what had become a semi-war zone. Yet our idea was to attract not "ordinary tourists" but rather those on "fact-finding missions"—journalists and politically interested groups—to "come and see." The guesthouse was an advocacy tool to tell the story of our people, to show our struggle, and to look for solidarity. This concept proved to be very successful, was copied by many organizations in Palestine, and became a game changer.

Then later, with the collapse of the peace process in the year 2000, Israeli tanks invaded our towns, including Bethlehem. Our own center (next to the church) was occupied by the Israeli army and partly damaged. Destruction was visible everywhere. Hope in justice was lost, and people were disillusioned with peace. The shattered glass on the streets was a symbol of the shattered hopes of the people. We again felt called to do something.[23]

We asked our students to go out into the streets, to gather the broken pieces of glass, to bring them into our workshops, and to make them into

23. Mitri Raheb, *Bethlehem Besieged: Stories of Hope in Times of Trouble* (Minneapolis: Fortress, 2004).

art pieces. Some did crosses, others did angels, others did doves. The idea was to transform the symbols of destruction into symbols of beauty, to change symbols of death into symbols of life. At the destroyed entrance to our center in downtown Bethlehem, we hung a huge piece of black cloth like a vertical banner and wrote on it in white, "Destruction may be . . . Continuity Shall be." Our message was that the destruction and evil forces can't force us to give up hope or leave.

On the contrary, when everything seemed to be lost, it was time for us to invest in our town. In this context, we decided to launch the first Lutheran university in the Middle East, Dar al-Kalima University College of Arts and Culture.[24] This was a kind of statement of hope that we will not give up on our city or on our rights. It was also a statement of commitment to our community. When so much was lost, we felt the need to plant an apple or, even better, an olive tree. We needed to invest in educating the next generation of creative leaders for Palestine. We felt that the best contribution a small Lutheran congregation can make is to help shape the art and cultural scene in Palestine. We felt that the political tide was against us, but we needed to train the next generation of visual artists, filmmakers, musicians, actors, and designers who could carve a different future for Palestine. People thought we were crazy to embark on such a huge task at that grim moment. But this was a statement of faith: hope in action. And today, this university that was started in the crypt of the church has a state-of-the-art campus. It is a city on a hill that cannot be hidden. Our students have become agents of change in the society. Their films are screened at Cannes Film Festival, their performances are getting noticed, and their designs are changing the face of the city. In their works, they give a human face to our people and struggle, they advocate for gender justice, and they present songs of hope and courage.

We find ourselves today at a junction of world history where voices of fascism, religious extremism, and exclusive nationalisms are on the rise. We are experiencing violations of human rights, a questioning of the role of international law, and an erosion of human values while countries in the Global South continue to be exploited. "And though this world with devils filled . . ." This stanza summarizes best Luther's biography and context—as well as ours as Palestinians. We need to free the Bible and theology from its "white-privileged captivity." The three solas rightly understood provide three important keys to understand the Scripture as texts of resistance to oppressions, grace as a call to liberation from religious terror, and hope as faith in action in the face of atrocities and despair. A rediscovery of Luther's solas based on the experience of the Global South can utilize

24. Dar al-Kalima University College of Arts and Culture (website), 2016, https://www.daralkalima.edu.ps.

the Bible as texts of resistance to empire rules, settler colonialism, wars, military, and surveillance activities on civilian populations. It can shed new light on sola gratia as a call to liberation from religious domination that continues to erase civil liberties across the world, while the sola spes reminds the faithful of our intellectual responsibility and faith commitment toward the world's social and cultural concerns.

STUDY QUESTIONS

1. How do Scripture and Lutheran theology help the people of Palestine sustain hope?
2. Read together the words of the founding members of the CAFCAW (pgs. 52–53). What stands out to you in their confession of faith?
3. Raheb writes, "Hope is what we do today even though the world might come to an end tomorrow." What actions does hope in the future that God has promised lead the church to today? How does the church reflect hope in a world that can so often seem hopeless?

5.

Polarization in Our Parishes, Societies, and World Today

Can Luther Help?

KAREN L. BLOOMQUIST

At first glance, Martin Luther seems an unlikely candidate to counter the increasing polarization and populism that have become characteristic of our times! After all, some historians claim he fueled much of the populism of his day, especially by using the printing press, the new social media of that time. His anti-Catholic, anti-Jewish, anti-"Turk" (Muslim) words and stances contributed to polarizing rhetoric. Many have viewed his legacy as providing the basis of what has been the spread of "evangelical" and right-wing churches around the world.

Indeed, Luther was quite a polarizing figure; people either loved or hated him. Fortunately, however, this polarization has begun to change with the warming of ecumenical relationships over the past fifty years, especially with the signing in 1999 of the Joint Declaration on the Doctrine of Justification with the Catholic Church. Although some of Luther's polarizing rhetoric was probably even worse than what we hear today, the *systemic* changes he advocated for, both for the church and for the society of his day, were revolutionary. They resulted in many changes in society, especially in northern Europe. This influence is one reason the Reformation movement caught on and has spread in many places around the world.

These social reforms have usually been thought of as occurring in the civil realm. The realm of salvation is rooted in the good news of what God has done through Jesus Christ and not what we do in society for sake of the neighbor. However, it is through this good news that we are freed to serve neighbors throughout the world. This includes how we personally help the neighbor but also what we do collectively to ensure that structures and policies safeguard a sufficient, sustainable livelihood for all. The church's public voice and actions are needed in collaboration with others in civil society. Certainly this is crucial in times, such as now, when governments around the world too often neglect their responsibility for the common good of all people. This influence of Luther has often been forgotten, and those following him have too often been quiet—supportive of the powers ruling in society rather than public in their protest against injustice and corruption. Lutherans have tended to keep to themselves, in private realms.

But is this sufficient? Today, we face a deeply spiritual crisis that must be addressed in theological terms that go beyond what has been the binary "two kingdoms" framework that Lutherans have inherited. We need to break out of the usual separation of what is spiritual and secular in order to address what is driving those who are attracted to polarizing populist appeals. This has to do with whole worldviews and people's fears and deep identity, and it needs to be addressed in these terms.

There is no straight line between Luther's time and ours, nor in his responses. His usual answers may not suffice today. For example, the lock he picked with the doctrine of justification may not be what is holding people in bondage today. In Luther's time, nearly everyone felt dependent on God. Today, when many in the West claim they no longer depend on or even believe in God, our situation is quite different.

Polarization is an epidemic not just in the United States but throughout the world. Behind the polarizing populism today are deeply spiritual and theological matters that have to do with worldview or logic—the whole way people are being formed today and their hoped-for future. In other words, it is a deeply spiritual rather than only a civil matter.

In the sixteenth century, the insightful Luther sensed what was holding people in bondage and swaying them. He addressed this bondage in an appealing way for common folk. It was popular! After all, he truly was a *contextual* theologian who addressed and engaged his context, one that was quite different from ours. The challenge is to be similarly contextual today. As Jesus provocatively says in Luke 12:56 NASB, "You do not know how to analyze this *present* time." Taking up this challenge here and now, we ask, Are there aspects of Luther's theology that can be imaginatively "transfigured" (familiar teachings or figures that in new settings acquire new meanings) and thus helpful for the challenges we face today?

THE ALLURE OF FEAR

David Brooks has said what now has become obvious:

> Fear pervades our society and sets the emotional tone for our politics. When historians define this era they may well see it above all else as a time defined by fear; an era when politicians rise by stoking fear. Fear generates fear. Everybody feels besieged—power is somehow elsewhere, with the malevolent forces who are somewhere out there, who will stop at nothing. Fear makes everything amorphous. But for those in the grip of fear, immigration—or globalization, Silicon Valley, Wall Street or automation—are shapeless, insidious forces that are out of control. The inevitable reaction is overreaction. Fear stokes anger, which then stokes more fear.[1]

I would add, fear is a big factor contributing to much of the allure of populist appeals and the resulting polarization today.

As Martha Nussbaum has written in *The Monarchy of Fear*, "Fear, indeed, is intensely narcissistic. . . . It drives out all thoughts of others."[2] The fearful person doesn't see particular individuals, just hateful shades who arouse disgust and can be blamed. Muslims are disgusting. Immigrants are disgusting. Republicans are disgusting. Fear induces herding behavior. The irrationalities of disgust underlie many social evils.

Fear also was pervasive in Luther's time. Fear of judgment, especially from God, of the devil, of the end-times. His theology was developed in response to such fears and how they had overtaken people. Fear had become an existential matter; it was the reigning worldview, controlling much of life. It is deeply connected with Luther's Christology and his view of God.

Much of this has been unearthed and provocatively reenvisioned by the late Vítor Westhelle, who suggested that those who are marginalized are especially those who dwell in the promise of the hoped-for future. Therefore, Westhelle posits, crises in society ought to be set within this wider framework. Rather than God's promised fulfillment of all as what we look forward to after we die, the hope of this fulfillment is embedded in everyday life and how we view *everything*—not as those who remain captive to fear but as those living by promise. It is about remembering and framing hope amid lament. The philosopher Walter Benjamin has stated, "In remembrance we have an experience that forbids us to conceive of history as a-theological."[3]

1. David Brooks, "An Era Defined by Fear," *New York Times*, April 29, 2019, https://tinyurl.com/437upet9.

2. Martha Nussbaum, *The Monarchy of Fear: A Philosopher Looks at Our Political Crisis* (New York: Simon & Schuster, 2018), 29.

3. Vítor Westhelle, *After Heresy* (Eugene, OR: Wipf & Stock, 2010), 137.

Yet today, history and future hope are usually devoid of any over-arching theological meaning. There is no universal history as may have been the case in previous eras. Much of this has been challenged because of the resulting domination. The contexts—and the significance of space and time—do matter, especially in a globalized world that takes local contexts seriously. So are we left with only fragments based on identity and nationalism? The new upsurge of nationalism seems to be driven by a hunger for identity, for a solid sense of one's presence in the world.[4] Is this where hope now is lodged? Can this be dislodged theologically in ways that avoid the dominating and homogenizing tendencies of the past? This is what churches and other faith communities are uniquely equipped to do. And the good news is that many people throughout the world are pursuing this, challenging what they have been taught in the past by missionaries and colonizers.

THE EMERGENCE OF IDENTITY

Admittedly, Luther did not yet have a modern understanding of the "self." In his time, belief and trust in God were a given. But for many today, those are not necessarily givens. He focused on the spiritual relationship (in which we do not do anything to deserve God's favor), which is quite different from what we do for the sake of the neighbor—through home, economic, community, and political activities. As the Evangelical Lutheran Church in America (ELCA) puts it, "God's work. Our hands." This has become the basis for much advocacy work, especially in the past fifty years. This continues to be the case and is more needed now than ever.

But is this sufficient in the strange times we live in? The self was set over and against the works-righteous other. This binary way of think-ing became an ideological weapon.[5] It has also fueled the polarization that now plagues society and permeates people's identity or sense of self.

Many developments have led to the modern rise of expressive indi-vidualism with persons choosing what is "authentic" for themselves—at least for those who have been educated, are of a higher strata, or are able to do such apart from institutional support. But for many others, their past history or their current ascribed status has inhibited this. They have been overlooked, marginalized, and discriminated against because of who they are. They do not fit the prevailing white, male, heterosexual, relatively affluent norm. Thus various recent movements have arisen that

4. Lewis Hyde, "How Nationalism Can Destroy a Nation," *New York Times*, August, 21, 2019, https://tinyurl.com/77sn6xnn.

5. Brigitte Kahl, "Justification, Ethics and the 'Other,'" in *Luther, Bonhoeffer, and Public Ethics*, ed. Michael P. DeJonge and Clifford J. Green (Lanham, MD: Lexington, 2019), 68.

are rooted in these identities: "This is who I am, and I'm proud of it!" These movements have achieved much and have been positive developments in this society, especially in the *intersectionality* of these identities, here and throughout the world. This has, for example, contributed to the growth of Lutheran churches in the Global South, such as in parts of Africa and among the Dalits in India. They especially have sensed the liberating heart of Lutheran theology. Over the past half century, the Lutheran World Federation (LWF) has especially contributed to this. There is a widespread sense that at least there is more tolerance (or so we have assumed!), although inequalities and various forms of discrimination remain.

But not all have been caught up in these movements. Many are attracted to other appeals. They continue to feel left out, perhaps even more so as they view these groups that seem to be "moving up." They often feel stuck in the working class or in poverty. They often wonder, *Where is "my" identity when it no longer is rooted in a relatively homogeneous identity?* (as if America ever had this). They increasingly feel forgotten in a society that has become progressively more diverse and, more and more, where "democracy" is being siloed into identity politics, which may be radically changing if not destroying democracy as we have known it.

IDENTITY POLITICS TODAY

Until recently, politics has been explained in terms of *economic* interests. Which groups are benefiting or not from an economic system or policies? This is still largely the case, even though amazement is expressed that people often vote or support policies that are counter to their interests. Rather than politics being driven by economic concerns, something else is driving political developments today—namely, "identity politics."

Identity politics is important and good, insofar as it raises up for public recognition groups of people who long have been marginalized, discriminated against, or treated unjustly. This has especially been occurring in terms of those who are African American, part of various ethnic groups, women, and people who identify themselves as gay, lesbian, trans, and so on. This now is reflected in much education, media, and public discourse. This becomes the basis of organizing for collective action and political appeals. Identity politics becomes the basis for protest or resistance. This is important, but it does not usually result in changed policies that effectively lessen economic disparities.

However, some inevitably feel left out when identity politics reigns, especially those who don't identify with one of these groups or even resent how others are being raised up or advanced. They begin to feel like "strangers in their own land" (the title of Arlie Hochschild's book), invisible or passed over. This has been occurring over some decades. For them, the "American dream" has become a "dream betrayed" (as I maintained in my 1990 book *The Dream Betrayed: Religious Challenge of the Working Class*).

Furthermore, this may have led to a "democratic recession" in which politics is no longer in terms of *economic* policies traditionally associated with the Left or the Right but in terms of *identity* interests on the Left, of the marginalized for justice, and on the Right, of patriotism and nationalism. People may even be attracted by what actually is against their economic advantage. Instead, they identify with "their group." Increasingly, politics has become polarized in these terms, and this has fed into much of the populism and nationalism that now is raging around the world. With identity issues, "either you recognize me, or you don't." Resentment over lost dignity or invisibility often has economic roots, but as Francis Fukuyama has pointed out, "Fights over identity often distract us from focusing on policies that could actually remedy those issues. . . . Social media has succeeded in accelerating the fragmentation of liberal societies by playing into the hand of identity groups."[6]

People are motivated by *more* than economic interests—desires for dignity, respect, and being "better" or "superior" to others. Even though the demand for recognition often is satisfied through economic means, politics today is weakly related to economic resources. Interestingly, the political scientist Fukuyama turns first to Luther's "valorizing the inner self over the external social being"[7] such that society itself (and for Luther, the church) has to adjust to the demands of the inner person. This led not only to the Protestant Reformation opposing practices required by the church of that day but also to various other developments that prioritized individual believers over prevailing social structures.[8] Historically, this has also led to many subsequent revolutions and wars. On the one hand, individual rights have become more universally recognized, and on the other hand, various identity-based nationalisms continued to spread and especially do so today.

CAN LUTHER HELP?

Luther was motivated by a yearning for greater justice for those left behind, which often has not been appreciated but which the previous *Forgotten Luther* books have rightly raised up. Yet Luther did not consistently back the peasants and their struggle then! In many places around

---

6. Francis Fukuyama, *Identity: The Demand for Dignity and the Politics of Resentment* (New York: Farrar, Straus and Giroux, 2018), 179–80.

7. Fukuyama, 26.

8. Fukuyama, 27.

the world today, the "peasant wars" continue. Might there be something in what Luther unleashed theologically in the sixteenth century that would be helpful in countering and transforming the polarizations that have been growing throughout the world today?

Where, really, is our identity rooted? For Luther, this was based on the assumption that everyone was Christian—which is certainly not the case in most interfaith contexts today. Although historically, Luther's anti-Jewish and anti-Islamic tendencies must be denounced, the implications of identity that is rooted in the inner self, and thus the dignity of all persons, must be raised up rather than what today have become the polarizing tendencies of identity politics. What is at stake first is a matter of theological anthropology—of how identity is conceived—not of politics, although it now is deeply infecting what is happening today in the political realm.

Luther stridently countered what was occurring in church and society in his day. In that sense, we need to be more like him! He was not reluctant to publicly address such—yet drawing directly on some of his biting words can increase the polarizing occurring today. At the heart of his theology, something else was going on that can speak to the heart of what ails us today. He boldly reframed matters, as must we today, in ways that go beyond polarization.

Rather than only personalizing attacks, Luther actually was addressing a far more pervasive *systemic* matter. Rather than some persons being good and others evil, he insisted that each of us is simultaneously saint and sinner (*simil iustus et peccator*). What is evil or "of the devil" cannot be attached to a person. As John Swinton has written, "Evil is not something that 'others' do; it is something that each of us has the potential to become involved with."[9] Persons are often labeled today as good or evil, righteous or unrighteous, sinful or good. But these are deeply intertwined in each of us and cannot be personally polarized, especially in quest of moral purity or "being better than others." This quest for moral purity is one of the factors leading to polarization. "I am right and more morally pure than is the other side." (This can be from the self-righteous Left as well as the Right.) Collaborating with those on the other side is taboo. At the same time, however, this does not preclude some positions or policies that must publicly be declared as immoral or unjust because of their effect on especially the most vulnerable neighbors. Here we must be inspired by Luther!

9. John Swinton, *Raging with Compassion: Pastoral Responses to Problem of Evil* (Grand Rapids, MI: Eerdmans, 2007), 68.

OUR IDENTITY IS FORMED IN RELATION TO OTHERS

How we are transformed with those who are other from us is poignantly expressed in Luther's theology of the Eucharist: "The sacrament has no blessing and significance unless love grows daily and so changes a person that he is made one with all others. . . . We become one loaf, one bread, one body, one drink and have all things in common. . . . In this way we are changed into one another and are made into a community by love."[10]

This is far different from the identity politics that is threatening democracies today. For Luther, there is a deep sense that we live not in and for ourselves. We are set outside ourselves and have faith or trust in God instead. We live not in ourselves but in Christ by faith and thus for the neighbor in love. Being self-absorbed, turned in only on oneself, is the essence of sin. Luther advocates a both/and approach, the self *and* the other (the neighbor). Our identity is not something we achieve or work out by what we do. Self and neighbor are intertwined in our identity. Although for Luther, God is fundamental to every constitution of the self, some today say they do not depend on God. Nevertheless, they, too, are closely related to those considered "other" and with whom they reciprocally relate. The self is essentially relational, not in competition with or over and against others. Many recently have expanded on this. Movements today assume this, as do many cultures throughout the world, which is why intersectionality in organizing with those who are different has become so crucial.

The New Testament scholar Brigitte Kahl focuses on the Letter to the Galatians and proposes that it is a wrong reading to juxtapose law and faith, as Lutheran justification theology often does, because this establishes a righteous self in opposition to an unrighteous other. This results in God supporting the superior and in-group position of the (Christian/Protestant) self over and against the inferior and outcast other. This establishes the Western Christian self that is entitled to conquer, rule, exploit, and even exterminate the other. This construct is idolatrous. It makes the self not only self-righteous but also godlike; it contradicts the messianic logic of the cross, where God appears as the other and with the other—that is, on the side of the sinner, the nobody, the weak. Kahl concludes that the theological core of the Letter to the Galatians is not a bipolarity of Jews versus Gentiles (or Christians), nor any other bipolarity, but rather Paul's visionary-apocalyptic insight that "in Christ," the dichotomies of the present world order are invalidated. The polarities between self and other, good and evil, righteous and unrighteous that establish the meaning,

10. Martin Luther, "Treatise concerning the Blessed Sacrament of the Holy and True Body of Christ and concerning the Brotherhoods," 1519, in *LW* 35:58.

identity, and social location of self and other in hierarchical and mutually exclusive arrangements are all vanishing in a new practice of becoming "one" *with* another rather than one *against* the other.[11]

CHURCH IS FORMED AROUND MORE
THAN IDENTITY MARKERS

Many of the current strategies for growing or revitalizing congregations draw heavily on ethnic/racial identities, class, identities, or age affinities. These may be based on who is moving into an area, those of a different class or job status or lifestyle than those who have lived there before or who are of a different generation. Appealing to these new groups *is* important; they may be looking for community that otherwise is lacking. Forming community with others is key in what it means to be church.

But if this only means drawing together those whose culture or origin is alike, or who may be of a similar status (affluent or poor) or age (young or old), or whose lifestyle and politics are similar, this can become a narrow, deficient way of being church. Relationships, and thus community, are formed across these differences, which constitute what it means to be the church. The early church often fell into this trap, which is why Paul insisted that, for example, there is neither Jew nor Greek. What is central in being the church is cutting across identity boundaries and the formation of a new community that is composed of those who have different identity markers. This goes against natural human tendencies, which, then and now, may be why many fail to understand what being "in Christ" really means: a new community composed of those who are quite different in their identities.

We cling to certain identities, which is why many immigrant communities have long established their own churches, often with their own language with which to worship, or even with their own ethnic tribe, so as to feel "at home" or "like a family." Certain cultural practices are perpetuated, which can be enriching to those involved but also keep out those who feel like outsiders. But this may be where it ends, not engaging others in the wider community and the public issues arising there. Instead, the "church" as it has been is pursued.

Unfortunately, that also has contributed to various kinds of polarization that pervade our current reality based on identities that are clung to, whether ethnic and racial, economic, generational, or political. Today, affiliating with those of another political commitment is even more

---

11. Brigitte Kahl, "Paul and the Law in Galatians: Roman Nomos or Jewish Torah?," in *Radicalizing Reformation*, ed. Karen L. Bloomquist, Craig Nessan, and Hans G. Ulrich (Zurich: LIT Verlag, 2016), 6:59–90.

scorned than it was previously with those of another race. Keeping with "one's own kind" is the tendency. *But that is not the Church!* Can we model something different in society, in ways that cut across and transform polarizing tendencies?

What is needed now are renewed theologically based understandings of what it means to be the church, involving especially those who remain on the fringes of churches or faith communities because they are skeptical of what it really means to be church today, in ways that go beyond institutional self-preservation and in which they do not want to participate.

A RELATIONAL, TRINITARIAN WORLDVIEW

The Brazilian liberation theologian Leonardo Boff reminds us that the domination model must be replaced by the communion model.[12] In the communion model, dialogue, consensus, and seeking the common good together become the basic framework for living together. Collaborating and cooperating produce the common good (justice for all)—God is a community/communion. There is mutual acceptance of differences. The Spirit is at work transforming polarizing situations.

The chair of the graduate theology department (R. Sahayadhas) at United Theological College in Bangalore, India, has proposed in his recent book that Luther's view is strategic for countering the identity politics and polarization that are fueled in India by what is raging there as Hindu fundamentalism (Hindutva), which suspects those who are not Hindi. He points to the "perichoretic communion"[13] of differences and unity, an image of how God exists as Trinity. In this sense, the church is called to be a sign and transformation of this world. Identity is formed in relationship *with*, not over and against, others. Moralism is selfishly seeking self-purity and perfection and results in distinctions and differences rather than the dialectics characteristic of Luther's theology. Identity politics can stand in the way of real liberation of the marginalized.[14]

If polarization is rooted in an overall worldview or logic, might a Trinitarian theology transform this? The essential interrelated dance of the Trinity is indeed countercultural, and in that sense, it might help us move beyond the polarizations. This also may make a difference for those many today who have rejected a dominating, singular God.

As my congregational pastor (Jeff Johnson) answers when asked on the street, "Are you a Christian?" he responds, "I'm Lutheran." That really

---

12. Leonardo Boff, *Trinity and Society* (Maryknoll, NY: Orbis, 1988), 120.

13. R. Sahayadhas, *Hindu Nationalism and the Indian Church: Toward an Ecclesiology in Conversation with Martin Luther* (New Delhi: Christian World Imprints, 2016), 400.

14. Sahayadhas, 292.

befuddles many, especially those on the West Coast who don't have any idea what that means. When asked, "Do you believe in God?" and he responds, "I believe in the Trinity," they become even more befuddled.

SO WHAT MIGHT THIS ENTAIL IN OUR COMMUNITIES?

Some thirty years ago when the ELCA began, we raised up a "community of moral deliberation" as what we hoped would be a distinctive mark of this new church and produced resources to help with this, including around what then became divisive issues of sexuality. In light of the vicious forms of polarization that now are raging, this may seem like a naïve hope. Has talking with, much less deliberating with, those with whom we have strong differences even become possible today? If identity is rooted in positions we hold, or the group we identify with, the prospects for such are dismal. But if our identity is grounded in that which transcends the positions we hold or the group we identify with, we are empowered with others to seek the common good of all—not necessarily through compromising but through hearing those with whom we most disagree.

While I was staffing the development of the ELCA social statement on abortion (which was a polarizing topic then and now), the church being a community of moral deliberation was tested, with good results that have endured. The positions of those on the task force were quite different, but they began by sharing values they agreed on and moved from there to more divisive matters. What was key was reframing the debate in ways that went beyond the usual pro-life versus pro-choice positions—although the media still tried (inaccurately) to cast it in these polarizing terms.

In the give-and-take process, and the resulting deeper connecting, there can be a ferreting out of ideological assumptions of those who differ, as we together search for what is faithful to what God intends. We need what the experience and insights of the other can bring so that through them, the "otherness" of biblical texts might speak in new ways to us. In this Spirit-empowered process, our sense of "we" is bound to be transformed; we can no longer think of "us" in ways that stand against "others." It is through this that a more authentic and credible public position is likely to emerge, one that incorporates a variety of perspectives and thus is pluralistic rather than monolithically driven by ideological differences or identities. Differences are *constitutive* of unity or connectedness that is theologically grounded for the sake of the world.[15]

---

15. Sahayadhas, 89.

Discernment involves eyes, ears, minds, hearts, bodies, experiences, feelings, stories, histories, and more. What is especially crucial is honoring what is seen or remembered by those who are often left out. Far more is at stake than a renewing of minds, understood in a narrow sense. Active discernment necessarily occurs in community with others, which helps keep us humble. How we see, feel, and evaluate our faith and ethical convictions begins to be transformed—not speaking, but listening, being transformed by the other and living this out through our commitments and actions, in other words, *enacting* communion, not just talking about it.

To conclude, yes, there is hope (rooted in our theology) for transforming the currently raging polarizations, drawing on what the church and other faith communities have long been about—not at the periphery but out of the heart of a faith that is lodged elsewhere. As those inspired by Luther, we need to be bolder in doing that more publicly in our congregations, communities, and world.

STUDY QUESTIONS

1. Bloomquist identifies fear as a significant source of division in society today. What fears might be keeping people divided? How might Luther's teachings and faith help us deal with the reality of fear in our world today?
2. We all have a sense of personal identity. Bloomquist discusses how our common need for identity can become lost in the political and social polarizing forces that clamor for our allegiance—overwhelming and even compromising the "identity" we find in our Christian faith. How do you experience this tension in your own life and in your church?
3. How does Bloomquist suggest the forgotten Luther might help Christians witness to a world divided by fear and identity?

6.

When Politics Fails and Disappoints
Citizenship Formation and the Role of the Church

GUILLERMO HANSEN

INTRODUCTION

Since 2016, we find ourselves in the United States immersed in a bizarre scenario. Words that formerly were uttered in relation to obscure regimes long bygone or in reference to distant "Third World" countries—*authoritarianism*, *fascism*, and *populism*—crowd our tweets, social media comments, and the news. Something monumental is happening in what once was considered the stronghold of liberal democracy, tolerance, and pluralism. This perceived liberal culture and ethos seem now to be under siege, engulfed in so-called illiberal trends and movements. Hopefully, this crisis will serve to invigorate democracy and lead to a reenchantment with politics. But the opposite may also be the case: the falling into a disenchantment or resignation with politics in general and democracy in particular, opening a dangerous scenario for more inequality, social injustice, and ecological degradation.

If anything, recent events reveal two things: first, that our American democratic manifest destiny is a delusion and, second, that undemocratic and illiberal currents are as American as apple pie. This problematic, of course, has historical, economic, and institutional components that must eventually be faced. But it also has a dimension that is more difficult to address: *What is going on in people's minds?*

It is too tempting to blame our crisis on the wicked character of politicians and government. We spontaneously do this instead of understanding this crisis as a symptom of a larger sociocultural dislocation lodged at the core of civil society. Structural, institutional, and economic approaches are always necessary for understanding politics and for love to be effective in the social field. Yet in doing so, we must dig deep into the realm of the human (social) mind and particularly into the ways in which values and modes of perception are structured around root metaphors and framing models. Values never exist in abstraction but are embedded in larger cognitive constructions that guide our understanding of reality. How are these values and perceptions formed?

I approach these themes on the basis of personal and social experiences that led me to appreciate the invaluable role of the church as a space of spiritual formation, particularly in times of social and cultural disruptions. I come from a country, Argentina, that in its modern history has swayed between authoritarian/dictatorial regimes and democracy with populism appearing as a "saving" mediation. It is a country that despite its natural and human wealth seems entrapped in a cyclical course. In attempting to track the roots of the crisis, we became experts in economic theories, socioanalytical tools, historiography, and cultural anthropology. But there was one dimension always left behind: the cognitive aspects—the feelings, experiences, and thoughts that shape the imaginary of citizenship and, eventually, democracy. In other words, the subjective disposition that leads to healthy and flourishing political engagement.

It is said that the events experienced in late adolescence and early adulthood will mark much of your political thinking.[1] In the Argentina of the 1970s and 1980s, these formative experiences included living under a "state of exception" where the law guaranteeing civil liberties and democratic processes was indefinitely suspended without being abrogated. The experience of military dictatorship, with its systematic violations of human rights and forced "disappearances" in order to safeguard "Western-Christian civilization," constituted the background for my engagement with the struggle for human rights (through ecumenical organizations) and for the return of democracy (through political activism).

This militant praxis opened my eyes to realities that were far from my daily life, and since then, I have understood the vital role of politics for the defense and flourishing of life: *politics as an act of love.* But praxis is not just a societal activity seeking structural transformations and justice. It is also a consciousness or a cognitive mapping arranged around a constellation of values and ideas. In other words, the formation of a different consciousness is initially at odds with the larger environment, producing a kind of a cognitive short circuit. For me, the space for this short-circuiting was the church—a "spiritual lab" that kindled my social and political

---

1. See Greg Lukianoff and Jonathan Haidt, *The Coddling of the American Mind: How Good Intentions and Bad Ideas Are Setting Up a Generation for Failure* (New York: Penguin, 2018), Kindle. See also Peter Beinart, "The Lost Generation," *Atlantic* 324, no. 4 (October 1, 2019): 28.

vocation. Church was a place where I learned to become a citizen and a neighbor to others. In order to do so, the avalanche of propaganda and ideological distortion that we confronted daily in the classroom, on TV, and in newspapers had to be deconstructed. And that meant wrestling not only with politics but with religion as well.

Of course, university and family also played very important roles next to the church. These spaces provided anchors for a dissonance with my larger context, the sociocultural fabric of Argentina. This context was the result of four dominant forces: a Hispanic heritage prone to authoritarianism and disregard for the law, an oligarchic liberalism more prominent in the economic than the political field, a nationalist-populist movement in the form of Peronism, and the hegemonic Roman Catholic corporatist view of social life. Needless to say, none of these forces created the conditions for a robust civic life and a democratic consciousness. In my case, it was the Lutheran "code" that led me to short-circuit my surrounding context by acquiring the practices of tolerance, respect, and a high valuation of pluralism and human rights.[2]

POLITICS AND RELIGION: THE NATIONAL SECURITY DOCTRINE

The National Security Doctrine,[3] which informed the suspension of constitutional rights and civil liberties during Argentina's last dictatorship (1976–83), was a monumental example of how authoritarian "thin" ideologies require the "thick" description provided by dimensions of culture such as religion in order to gain legitimacy and traction in civil society.[4] This "doctrine" was the consequence of the marriage between US hemispheric policies of the 1960s and 1970s and local forms of nationalism articulated by Catholic integralism.[5] They joined forces in order to combat the threat of "communism"—an umbrella term that included not only communist and socialist militants but also trade unions, human rights groups, church

2. Of course, hundreds if not thousands of different organizations in civil society also played for others a similar role. I am not claiming any privileged position for the church, just referencing my experience.

3. See *Nunca Mas: The Report of the Argentine National Commission on the Disappeared*, with an introduction by Ronald Dworkin (New York: Farrar, Straus and Giroux, 1986), 442–45; David Rock, *Argentina (1516–1987): From Spanish Colonization to Alfonsín* (Berkeley: University of California Press, 1987), 376; and Iain Guest, *Behind the Disappearances: Argentina's Dirty War against Human Rights and the United Nations* (Philadelphia: University of Pennsylvania Press, 1990).

4. Cf. Andrew Arato and Jean Cohen, "Civil Society, Populism and Religion," *Constellations: An International Journal of Critical and Democratic Theory* 24, no. 3 (September 2017): 286.

5. See Fortunato Mallimaci, "El Catolicismo latinoamericano a fines del milenio: Incertidumbres desde el Cono Sur," *Nueva Sociedad* 136 (1995): 154–76.

leaders, and democratic organizations that questioned the imbalances of power and sought the empowerment of the subaltern social classes.

This doctrine was crystallized during the Nixon era and responded to the geopolitical experiences gained during the war in Vietnam. After the American defeat, a new strategy for containing "communism" developed in the Western Hemisphere that deputized the Latin American military and ruling classes to serve as the gendarmes of US hemispheric policies. Religion was a pivotal cultural substrate that would legitimize a generalized repression by wedding the notion of capitalism, democracy, and Western Christian civilization. It is one thing to resist communism in the name of political or economic abstractions, another to see resistance to communism as a crusade against "atheism." The National Security Doctrine was a continuation, through a different imperial power, of the toxic chemistry between greed and piety harkening back to the Spanish Requerimiento of the sixteenth and seventeenth centuries.[6]

The case was that a liberal democracy such as the United States actively carved out a state of exception to these values and institutions in its sphere of influence beyond its formal political boundaries. It was a matter of defending not a culture and political regime (*democracy*) but a system of economic extraction (*capitalism*). Suddenly, vast swaths of the Latin American population became *homo sacer*, accursed and persecuted.[7] Citizens were stripped of their rights and autonomy in the name of democracy and freedom. The existential fear of "communism" led to the formation of a subjective profile of the securitized: the gradual development of a voluntary servitude where we became not only objects of security but also its subjects. The Nazi regime in Europe and McCarthyism in the United States, with their encouragement of denunciations and constant vigilance, give an idea of the situation we faced. But with an added twist: Christianity itself was said to be at stake in this struggle. Hence for us, the critique of politics had to include a critique of religion, at least the form of religion that was being used to justify dictatorships, repression, and torture.

6. Cf. Raj Patel and Jason Moore, *A History of the World in Seven Cheap Things: A Guide to Capitalism, Nature, and the Future of the Planet* (Oakland, CA: California University Press, 2017), 94.

7. In *Stato di eccezione*, the Italian philosopher Giorgio Agamben shows how Western democracies become invested with the need of turning emergency into the foundation of their existence, on the basis of a new vigilance prompted by new definitions of who are the "accursed," the *homo sacer*. Giorgio Agamben, *Stato di eccezione* (Torino, Italy: Bollati Boringhieri, 2003), 37.

THE RUTHLESS CRITICISM OF EVERYTHING EXISTING

The collusion between a political strategy of repression and Catholic integralism[8] is what opened, in my experience, a chapter of rediscovering the potential for the critical and constructive consciousness to be found in a Lutheran understanding of power, politics, and economics. This was a form of Lutheranism that encouraged the use of "reason" and learning from the world in matters where it knows best. For example, Karl Marx helped us understand how political power is entrenched in economic interests and class divisions and leads to a distorted consciousness that accepts the prevailing conditions under a "mystical consciousness." Thus he spoke of a reform of consciousness that necessarily had to address simultaneously the religious and the political. In 1843, he wrote,

> The reform of consciousness consists *only* in enabling the world to clarify its consciousness, in waking it from its dream about itself, in *explaining* to it the meaning of its own actions. Our whole task can consist only in putting religious and political questions into self-conscious human form. . . . Our motto must therefore be: reform of consciousness not through dogmas, but through analyzing the mystical consciousness, the consciousness which is unclear to itself, whether it appears in religious or political form. . . . So, we can express the trend of our journal in one word: the work of our time to clarify to itself (critical philosophy) the meaning of its own struggle and its own desires. This is work for the world and for us. It can only be the work of joint forces. It is a matter of *confession*, no more. To have its sins forgiven mankind has only to declare them to be what they really are.[9]

Note that here Marx links the notion of critical consciousness with the very religious concept of confession and forgiveness of sins. In a way, it parallels Bonhoeffer's calling the church under the Nazi regime of his time to a "confessing moment"—a naming of the alien (Nazi) ideology that has slipped through the cracks of the church, perverting not only its witness but also the core of the gospel, Christ.[10] In Marx's case, this confession was secular and confronts the mystifying ideologies (religious and political) that have slipped in the world through the cracks of distorted economic relations.

8. It must be noted that I am referring to the hegemonic aspects of Catholicism, not to its alternative versions as expressed by progressive Catholicism, liberation theology, base ecclesial communities, and so on.

9. Karl Marx, "For a Ruthless Criticism of Everything Existing," in *The Marx-Engels Reader*, ed. Robert C. Tucker, 2nd ed. (New York: W. W. Norton, 1978), 15. This is a letter written in 1843 addressed to his fellow left-wing Hegelian Arnold Ruge.

10. See Dietrich Bonhoeffer, "The Jewish Christian Question as Status Confessionis," in *Dietrich Bonhoeffer Works*, ed. Larry L. Rasmussen, trans. Isabel Best, David Higgins, and Douglas W. Stott, vol. 12, *Berlin: 1932–1933* (Minneapolis: Fortress, 2009), 372.

The main point I want to draw, and that in part mirrors the process that churches under dictatorships had to face, is that in order to engage in democratic processes and civil discourse and action, a new consciousness is necessary. Much has contributed to the brainwashing, if not numbing, of minds in pursuing the disciplining of bodies. What type of transformation has to take place in order to change a mental mapping that, for example, tells you that you are guilty until proven innocent? Or that tells you that bodies and minds can be tortured for extracting information, enabling more torturing and persecution in the future? Certainly institutional, legislative, and procedural dimensions as well as economic relations had to be transformed for democracy to really work. But how can you transform these without also transforming consciousness? Barring another dictatorship, this time from the left, the long road to democracy and human rights necessitates something more radical. It necessitates a change in our subjectivities, in the ways in which we think and feel, and in the ways in which we tell our stories.

As we read Marx, and many others as well, we found ourselves engaged in a first "spiritual" step of a process that began with a critical accent wrapped in a confession of sin. Theologically, this can be interpreted as God's law in the form of a critical accusation,[11] which secularly translates as the necessary social critique that leads to a new imagined world. The fact that religion and politics are the main forms in which we human beings express our understanding of what we dream, struggle for, and desire[12] implies that the values that are expressed in these constellations relate to similar emotional and cognitive connections. That religion, through its stories, rituals, and codified beliefs, plays the emotional strings of our souls is not surprising. What can be a little more surprising is that politics also rests on its capacity to mobilize emotions.[13] Feelings are not the opposite of rationality; in fact, they embody evolutionary rationality.

A COGNITIVE APPROACH

Marx's call to reform consciousness, therefore, is a call to tackle the political and religious symbols that create the mystical consciousness that can be life giving or death dealing. But how does one gain this (critical) consciousness? How is it formed? It was not until much later that I understood how political and religious ideas and values are constructed around similar

11. Cf. Robert Bertram's understanding of the Lutheran conception of law as "divine criticism." *A Time for Confessing*, ed. Michael Hoy (Grand Rapids, MI: Eerdmans, 2008), 17.

12. See Martin Hägglund, *This Life: Secular Faith and Spiritual Freedom* (New York: Pantheon, 2019), 333.

13. See Yuval Harari, *21 Lessons for the 21st Century* (New York: Spiegel & Grau, 2018), Kindle.

paradigms, which in part explained how religious formulations are mapped into politics. Enter the field of cognitive studies.

Since the 1990s, a new interdisciplinary approach has coalesced around the general rubric of "cognitive studies." Religion has been one of its main areas of research, but politics quickly became an object of investigation as well. The presupposition is that both the political mind as well as the religious mind draws from the same basic cognitive structure that underlies the symbolic and metaphorical operation of the human mind. What we believe (transcendent or immanent) is directly related to how we think, and this remains largely unconscious. I am not saying that these two fields are the same (here the Lutheran doctrine of the two kingdoms is a healthy reminder of two different modes of the mind's operation) but that they significantly overlap. One result of this overlapping to the point of collusion is, precisely, the phenomenon of the National Security Doctrine in Latin American dictatorships, with its conflation of authoritarianism and nationalist Catholicism.

The American philosopher George Lakoff has explored the cognitive metaphors operating in political and religious constructs. His basic presupposition is that the mind (with its emotions, concepts, language, metaphors, etc.) is a thoroughly embodied process only understood in the larger framework of evolutionary theory and social life.[14] In Lakoff's theory, most of our knowledge and beliefs are framed in terms of conceptual systems that are lodged mostly in the cognitive unconscious. This is what shapes all aspects of our experience and can be initially understood by approaching the mind as an embodied phenomenon.

On this basis, Lakoff has analyzed not just the conceptual values that inform the "framing" of political and religious discourse but the edging of these narratives through models that order moral metaphors and valuations. While neither political nor religious life can be approached in a binary way, I find Lakoff's analysis of the basic patterns that lead to a conservative or progressive mind illuminating. Sophisticated and highly abstract ideologies, theologies, moralities, philosophies, and so on can be understood as different framings of primary and complex metaphors that are deeply entrenched in our embodied minds.

For Lakoff, there are two main models based on the *ideal of family life* that frame a series of metaphors leading to distinctive moral systems: the *strict father* model and the *nurturing parent* model. The use of family as a guiding metaphor for political and religious life is due to the fact that it is the first space in which we, as children, experience "governance" and power. These models conform narratives with dramatic structures (with

14. See George Lakoff and Mark Johnson, *Philosophy in the Flesh: The Embodied Mind and Its Challenges to Western Thought* (New York: Basic Books, 1999), 5–6.

archetypal roles like hero, villain, victim, helper, etc.), linking them to positive and negative emotional circuitries.[15] Narratives are thus mental structures deeply lodged in the bodily experiences of human beings, which in turn serve as templates for idealized national-political and religious life.

In the case of the strict father model, the main character is the father as a hero who confronts the perils and dangers of the world. He is the moral leader of the family, who in exchange for protection and support, demands obedience and discipline. The model assumes that life is a struggle for survival, so winning in the world becomes the main goal. Only a disciplined life can achieve that; therefore, punishment is necessary for equipping (children) to become self-reliant and prosperous in a very treacherous world. When this model is mapped into politics, "the strict father model explains why conservatism is concerned with authority, with obedience, with discipline, and with punishment. It makes sense in a patriarchal family where male strength dominates unquestionably."[16]

This model and narrative by which we live—as both an experience as well as a projection—also has a correlate in the religious world exemplified by a "strict Father Christianity," a cornerstone of the type of Roman Catholic integralism that we faced in Latin America (present-day "Evangelical" speech functions similarly). Here God (and/or his deputies) is imagined as the central hero of a plot that demands total obedience in exchange for which either earthly prosperity, a life of moral virtues, or heavenly rewards are promised. The narrative that arises is tethered by authority, obedience, discipline, and punishment.

The nurturing parent model of the family, on the other hand, emphasizes the equal responsibility of the caregivers without gender constraints. The job of the parental figures is to protect and empower children by nurturing them so they in turn may become nurturers of others. Nurturance is based on empathy, and discipline results not from punishment but from the child's growing sense of care and responsibility toward themselves, toward others, and toward the world. Restitution is preferred over punishment and mistakes, and error can be corrected by doing something right and making up for it. When this model is mapped onto the nation, the result is the progressive politics of protection, empowerment, and community.[17] In the religious field, the hero is either a crucified God or the triune community, God's nurturance is given freely and unconditionally, and what we receive (grace) empowers the nurturing of others in family, communities, society, politics, and the environment.

---

15. See George Lakoff, *The Political Mind: Why You Can't Understand 21st-Century American Politics with an 18th-Century Brain* (New York: Viking, 2008), 93.

16. Lakoff, 78.

17. Lakoff, 81.

In summary, the dictatorial and integralist metaphorical construct around the strict father model served, with its mythical and emotional appeal, to thicken the thin nature of dictatorships and authoritarian regimes. It allowed the framing of conservative tropes along key binary categorizations that, through complex metaphors, allow the expression of self-righteous indignation against the supposed perils besieging the nation, mobilize the "good" people, and demonize the foe. That the whole of Christian tradition can be framed through this constellation is, to say the least, one of the most calamitous developments in the recent history of the church in Latin America and elsewhere. But are there nurturing dimensions in the Christian narrative? Does it provide the symbolic language through which another way of being can be imagined and enacted?

A LUTHERAN CRITICAL
CONSCIOUSNESS AND SPIRITUALITY

As mentioned in the introduction, it was the church (with its spirituality and theology, rites and practices) that became for me a true "school of life." This does not mean that the church contained within itself all that is valuable in life, but that the gospel sent us to live with the command of living truly as the valued creatures we are. It taught us how religious faith cast in the Lutheran tradition can be transposed into a true secular faith affirming this life as the place for embodying a divine love for the sake of the neighbor. In other words, how the ultimate relates to the penultimate.[18]

As the Dutch anthropologist Geert Hofstede has shown, power distance, tolerance, and inclusion are key dimensions structuring any society and culture, and much of their meanings are acquired through family, school, workplace, and religious institutions.[19] Background theories, social experiences, and religious symbols and narratives set the parameters for a network of values (mythical-ethical core) where notions such as tolerance, respect, equality, and justice are forged, tested, denied, or embraced. What theological and spiritual resources do we possess in our Lutheran tradition to cultivate a nurturing attitude toward life in general and politics in particular?

It is my belief that Lutheranism possesses a decisive orientation toward the nurturing model. The doctrine of justification by faith, Paul's interpretation of Jesus's gospel as it reaches people in the margins (see 1 Cor

---

18. See Dietrich Bonhoeffer, "Ultimate and Penultimate Things," in *Dietrich Bonhoeffer Works*, ed. Ilse Tödt et al., vol. 6, *Ethics* (Minneapolis: Fortress, 2005), 145–70.

19. See Geert Hofstede, *Culture and Organizations: Software of the Mind* (New York: McGraw-Hill, 1997), 23–48.

1:26–29), is a key dimension in the way in which Lutheranism approaches the story of God. The doctrine, as formulated since Paul, is a critical and central guide to understanding the biblical message regarding the relationships between humans, creation, and God. It radically redraws the boundaries of God's domain in order to *include* those who hitherto were considered far from it: gentiles, slaves, women, urban poor, artisans, and people of doubtful religious orthodoxy. This inclusiveness is basic to all other doctrines and statements regarding Christian life. It leads to a gracious appraisal of the life of every person and creature, fueling generosity, imagination, patience, compassion, kindness, forgiveness, and loyalty (see 1 Cor 13).

In the same vein, Luther employed the language of justification to indicate that through Christ, God has made us equal participants in the justice revealed in Jesus. In this case, the "sinners"—which in the medieval scholastic distinction between a spiritual and secular state meant practically all of those who lived in the "world"—found a new space of inclusion. Luther could forcefully stress justification because this was central to a radical reformulation of God and God's intimate involvement with creation in general and human beings in particular. The language of justification expresses a strategy of inclusion of the destitute, the marginal, and the excluded, not into the logic of what exists, but into a new redistributive community of social, spiritual, and material goods.[20] This communicated the hidden character of God's rule and subverted the retributive traditions where God is represented as a powerful creditor.

In their respective ways, both Paul and Luther sought to translate into their contexts the normative dimension of Jesus's message about a merciful God, a generous kingdom, and his ministry of crossing the boundaries that separate human beings. In effect, justification encodes the multiple forms in which Jesus's ministry interweaves divine righteousness, social justice, and mercy. The gospel traditions emphasize Jesus crossed the traditional boundaries of family, honor and dishonor, Jews and Gentiles, men and women, sick and healthy, pure and impure, country and city, poor and rich. Bearing witness to God's mercy and coming reign, he embodies a new space: the space of the Spirit. His body, his words, and his presence become the locus for a new narrative that is not only about God but also about how God crosses over into the bodies and minds of those who never expected to be considered as somebodies. To draw boundaries is an act of disenfranchising power; to trespass them is an act of divine imagination and love.[21]

20. See Martin Luther, "Treatise concerning the Blessed Sacrament of the Holy and True Body of Christ and concerning the Brotherhoods," 1519, in *LW* 35:45–73.

21. See Guillermo Hansen, "On Boundaries and Bridges: Lutheran *Communio* and Catholicity," in *Between Vision and Reality: Lutheran Churches in Transition. LWF Documentation 47/2001,* ed. Wolfgang Greive (Geneva: Lutheran World Federation, 2001), 87–88.

Under the Argentine dictatorship, this notion of justification by grace through faith prompted in us a new consciousness where we saw our existence grounded no longer in us or in a defense of our nation or in Western values but in realities that were "external" to us: Christ and the neighbor.[22] It was a key factor in the deconstruction of the consciousness that the propaganda machine of the dictatorship forged in our minds. Furthermore, the transposition or mapping of this spiritual faith (Christ) into the secular domain (neighbor) led us to see that the struggle for human rights and democracy was one of the ways in which the Christian is called to live outside of herself. It led us to anchor our existential concerns to those persecuted by the dictatorial regime and to engaging in a structural transformation that dismantled the walls of power. Politics, in other words, is an act of "going out," an act of love.

But in order to transpose or map our faith into the secular, the spontaneous and emotional beliefs contained within the message of justification by faith needed a further theological tweak. Otherwise, a religious consciousness may run into Manichean dualisms or to enthusiastic perfectionist impulses. This is what prompted Luther to map the secular as the place for the enactment of Christian spirituality through the framing of God's twofold governance/regime (the so-called doctrine of the two kingdoms). In doing so, Luther was, in principle, correct, since he invited us to look seriously at the dynamics and realities that govern our secular existence. But we also realized that Luther's sixteenth-century German formulation carried the ambiguity proper to a time of transition between feudalism and modernity. This can be seen in his own formulation of God's twofold regime, where the kingdom of the right (spiritual governance) was formulated in *nurturing* terms (*gospel, grace, salvation, cross*) and the kingdom of the left (secular governance) was still framed through *strict father* metaphorical constructs (*law, sword, punishment, authority*). It was thanks to a "christologization" of Luther's doctrine of the two kingdoms (which we learned through Dietrich Bonhoeffer and liberation and feminist theologians) that a more coherent and critical model emerged for us.

Christian spirituality is primarily grounded in the affirmation that in Jesus Christ, God has taken human form. As Bonhoeffer asserts, "From now on it is no longer possible to conceive and understand humanity other than in Jesus Christ, nor God other than in the human form of Jesus Christ."[23] Spirituality is thus a con-formation of minds and bodies

---

22. See Martin Luther, "The Freedom of a Christian," in *Martin Luther's Basic Theological Writings*, ed. Timothy Lull, 2nd ed. (Minneapolis: Fortress, 2005), 408: "We conclude, therefore, that a Christian lives not in himself, but in Christ and in his neighbor. . . . He lives in Christ through faith, in his neighbor through love." Luther, 418.

23. Dietrich Bonhoeffer, "History and Good (2)," in Tödt et al., *Dietrich Bonhoeffer Works*, 6:253.

to God's true form, Jesus Christ, and it is in this Christ that the world in general and the sufferer in particular are vindicated as God's "place."[24]

Thus through every practice, gesture, sermon, and sacramental moment, we are giving expression to not just a set of beliefs but a mapping of the world, whose challenges must be faced through the appropriate political means. The church is a cognitive lab that seeks to evoke and reinforce a certain circuitry in the central nervous system of human beings, what the apostle Paul called to have the mind of Christ (Phil 2:5) and Bonhoeffer echoed with his central category of "con-formation [Gleichgestaltung] with the form of the new human being, Christ."[25] It is the embodiment of a cognitive pattern of evocations that is not limited to the church but rather seeks to recognize itself in our encounter with our neighbors in need.

This is the realm of the "spiritual" that does not seek a direct formation of the world by planning and programs, by applying directly to the world so-called Christian principles—this is what politics is for.[26] Rather, it seeks to draw bodies and minds into the unique form of the one who became human and walked among those whose lives truly need a neighbor (see Good Samaritan). This is the praxis of faith, and faith, from the point of view of cognitive studies, is the rerouting of neuronal connections that places our minds and bodies in a different web of relationships and opens the world as the "secular" place where God is sustaining and transforming life. Thus the spiritual is always—indirectly—political, and the distinction between the two must be maintained in order to preserve the integrity and efficacy of their means.

The role of theology provides a grammar—a sort of algorithmic device—for framing and uplifting the elements of a nurturing model. I am speaking of not any theology but the theology that is grounded in the God that takes form in Jesus of Nazareth and that is thematized around the tropes of God's unconditional gift (justification by grace through faith), God's critique and reaffirmation (the law-gospel distinction), the understanding of the relation between secular and spiritual existence (two regimes/kingdoms), and the awareness that humility, generosity, and compassion stem from our recognition that we are still paradoxical and incomplete persons (simultaneously justified and sinner). These "doctrines" guide the structure of root metaphors linking and reinforcing connections that recall the nurturing experiences of our bodies and minds. They evoke the unconditional acceptance of our existences that takes us out of

24. Dietrich Bonhoeffer, "Ethics as Formation," in Tödt et al., *Dietrich Bonhoeffer Works*, 6:97.

25. Dietrich Bonhoeffer, "God's Love and the Disintegration of the World," in Tödt et al., *Dietrich Bonhoeffer Works*, 6:322.

26. See Bonhoeffer, "Ethics as Formation," 93.

the metaphorical imprisonment of our own egos into the larger world of Christ and the neighbor. To be spiritual is thus to be politically engaged.

CONCLUSION

Failure in politics comes down to an inability to match a society's resources to its biggest opportunities and needs in an inclusive, fair, and egalitarian way.[27] To redress this failure, legislation, procedural measurements, reform, and even revolution are necessary. But it is equally true that the structural failures we face as a society are deeply entrenched in the root metaphors and models that arise in life and relationships—as values and commitments. It is a question about where our hearts lie; as Luther writes, "Anything on which your heart relies and depends, I say, that is really your God."[28] In other words, the transformation of consciousnesses (hearts) is an integral dimension of our larger sociopolitical praxis. We are always dealing with human beings whose subjectivity is always in process.

Ultimately, the question is about the clash between a patriarchal or nurturing model (of God, of where our hearts are) and the way in which the latter is mapped in our secular and daily lives. Little can be expected if old "strict father" metaphors prevail in the "mind" and imagination of civil society and continue to shape its practices, commitments, and values. Deconstruction—that is, the ruthless criticism of everything existing—starts at home in our churches, families, and schools. But the reconstruction is expressed in the ways in which we engage the world through effective political strategies.

STUDY QUESTIONS

1. Hansen describes the ways his faith helped shape his perspective on the political and social struggles he experienced in Argentina. How does your faith help shape your perspective on political and social struggles today?

2. Hansen writes that the "notion of justification by grace through faith prompted in us a new consciousness where we saw our existence grounded no longer in us or in a defense of our nation or in Western values but in realities that were 'external' to us: Christ and the neighbor" (pg. 79). What do you think Hansen

27. See James Fallows, "In the Fall of Rome, Good News for America," *Atlantic* 324, no. 4 (October 1, 2019): 21.

28. Martin Luther, *The Large Catechism*, in *The Book of Concord: The Confession of the Evangelical Lutheran Church*, ed. Robert Kolb and Timothy Wengert (Minneapolis: Fortress, 2000), 386.

means by a "new consciousness"? What does it mean to base our identity on Christ and the neighbor rather than ourselves, our nation, or other values?

3. Hansen argues that Scripture, reason, and conscience can help provide Christians with a new awareness or perspective that can guard against authoritarianism and tyranny. How does your faith—and your congregation—help you understand and confront injustice in the world? Should the congregation be a place where Christians learn more about situations of injustice and how to correct them?

7.

Martin Luther for the Life of the Church

RAFAEL MALPICA PADILLA

George Tillman Jr.'s film *Men of Honor* (2000), starring Robert De Niro and Cuba Gooding Jr., tells the story of Master Chief Petty Officer Carl Brashear, the first African American master diver and the first amputee master diver in the US Navy. The reason I mention this movie is to use one of the primary tasks of a navy diver as the framework for my conversation with you regarding Martin Luther: navy divers are trained to conduct salvage.

Many of the presenters at the Forgotten Luther seminars agree that one of the most relevant tasks for theologians and students of Luther today is to rescue him from his domestication. Luther is, indeed, a controversial figure. His positions on the Jews, the Turks, the Anabaptists—that is, the religious other—are questionable. We in the Lutheran communion have apologized to the Jewish and Anabaptist communities for such writings. It is difficult to forget his stance against the peasants who, inspired by the Reformation, rose to fight for (and claim) their agrarian rights and their freedom from the oppression by the nobles and landlords.[1] However, in the midst of these contradictions, we find the Luther that is ultimately concerned with the neighbor in need. In his works, we find a clarion call

---

1. In his 1525 writing *Against the Robbing and Murdering Hordes of Peasants*, Luther sought to instruct the rulers on how they were to "conduct themselves in these circumstances." Luther objected to their uprising, calling it a sin because (1) they were disobedient to the established order that demanded their obedience to their lords, (2) they used violence to stake their claim, and (3) they became blasphemers for their use of the gospel (including their interpretation of Genesis 1 and 2) as the basis for their claims. His infamous phrase is extremely difficult to understand: "Therefore let everyone who can, smite, slay and stab, secretly or openly, remembering that nothing can be more poisonous, hurtful or devilish than a rebel." See E. G. Rupp and Benjamin Drewery, *Martin Luther: Documents of Modern History* (London: Eduard Arnold, 1970), 121–26.

to be totally committed to the other. The freedom of the gospel pushes us to seek and serve God's vulnerable ones.

It was Dr. Walter Altmann,[2] former professor at the Escola Superior de Teologia (EST) in Sao Leopoldo, Brazil, who introduced me to the notion of freeing Luther. Luther has been the subject of thousands of scholarly research pursuits, and that is where we have kept him, in the world of academia. Altmann and other voices from the "Third World" began to explore Luther's response to his context of oppression and marginalization in order to find some *pistas* (clues) for the engagement of Lutheran churches in the liberation movements sweeping across the Global South. Medardo Gomez (El Salvador), Manas Buthelezi (South Africa), Gudina Tumsa (Ethiopia), Ishmael Noko (the Lutheran World Federation [LWF]), Victoria Cortez (Nicaragua), and Zephania Kameeta (Namibia) were some of the rebel voices. Their praxis was an invitation to dive into the depths of the ocean to salvage Luther and reappropriate him for the life of the church.[3]

Vítor Westhelle in his *Transfiguring Luther: The Planetary Promise of Luther's Theology*[4] further expands this notion of reappropriating Luther's persona. For Westhelle, it does not suffice to just contextualize Luther. To a certain extent, Professor Westhelle sees the relevance of Luther as speaking directly into our contexts. He calls for Luther's *viva vox* to become alive in our midst, serving as a deconstruction tool for his enslavement and domestication. In this transfiguration, Luther becomes the "critical mass"[5] element that generates the reaction leading to the expected change.[6] Transfiguration—"the procedure by which a figure from a given context has the potential for being a catalyst of experiences for other contexts, or when a figure from a given context embodies the spirit of a figure from another context"[7]—brings Luther from the darkness of old theological disputes to the limelight of a world stage that is searching for viable

---

2. Walter Altmann, *Confrontación y liberación: Una perspectiva Latinoamericana sobre Martín Lutero* (Buenos Aires: ISEDET, 1987).

3. In her magnum opus *God for Us*, Catherine Mowry LaCugna embarks on a mission to transform an obscure doctrine into an illuminating experience for the life of the church. She says, "The doctrine of the Trinity is ultimately a practical doctrine with radical consequences for Christian life." Catherine Mowry LaCugna, *God for Us: The Trinity and Christian Life* (New York: HarperCollins, 1991), 1.

4. See Vítor Westhelle, *Transfiguring Luther: The Planetary Promise of Luther's Theology* (Eugene, OR: Cascade, 2016), Kindle.

5. Critical mass is "the smallest amount of matter needed to produce a nuclear chain reaction." *Cambridge Dictionary*, s.v. "critical mass," accessed February 2, 2020, https://tinyurl.com/39gvlk3x.

6. In my experience of Lutheranism in the United States, both Luther and Jesus have been domesticated (embodied by the famous Lutheran quietism). While for the purpose of this symposium we focus our attention on Luther, this by no means should be construed as idolizing Luther and displacing Jesus.

7. Westhelle, *Transfiguring Luther*, loc. 4582 of 8598.

alternatives to the ravaging results of nativist and populist governments wreaking havoc in our communities. In this era of "posttruth," does Luther have something to tell us?

THE YOUNG ADULTS IN GLOBAL MISSION EXPERIENCE

In 1999, the Division for Global Mission of the Evangelical Lutheran Church in America (ELCA) initiated Young Adults in Global Mission (YAGM), a program for young adults, seeking to provide them a space for critical reflection and service. That year, ten participants served with Time for God in the United Kingdom. Since then, 1,121 young adults have participated in this initiative that offers the opportunity to be globally formed and globally informed. A recent survey among YAGM alumni shows that 30 percent have attended seminary upon their return from international service, and 37 percent serve in the nonprofit, education, and health-care sectors.

Like most young adults in the United States, these YAGM participants do not come into the program seeking a religious experience. What attracts them to the program is their passion for justice and their desire to make a difference in a troubled world. While they question the vitality of their local church's engagement in the world—in contrast—what they find in their host church and communities is a vision for church that sees itself as an agent for change, an agency that is rooted in the gospel.

During their interview and discernment process, I am given the opportunity to talk to them about their future experience, providing an overview of the theological framework that guides our global engagement. *Accompaniment* is rooted in the action-reflection methodology that emerged in Latin America after the Second Vatican Council, and as a lens and method, it opens the door to reappropriate some of the traditional themes in a theology of mission. It is this process of reappropriation and "transfiguration" that excites them about their future experiences: how to read Scripture, tradition, Luther, the church, and so on from the margins, from a non-Western hegemonic ideological construct.

It is said that most young adults describe themselves as "spiritual but not religious." This "mantra" is challenged by the experience of "church" they find in the life of our companion churches, a church that exists for the sake of others. The YAGM experience assists them in understanding and addressing the dissonance between the church's discourse of itself—in the North American experience—and its practice. The key missiological question we face today is, "How do we engage the other?" and conversely, "How are we engaged by the other?" Luther's hermeneutical principle of neighbor love or the neighbor in need is critical in reassessing the missional task for the church today. Luther's neighbor love is a formidable appropriation of the Cappadocian[8] understanding of the essence of the Trinity: a community sustained by love, living in "extreme relationality" (its triunity). It is this essence (relationships as essence) that God wills for God's world. The notion of a church that exists for the sake of the world, for the neighbor in need, and not to build its institutional capacity captures their imagination and gives them a sense of meaning and purpose. This is consistent with what research says about millennials: "Millennials tend to see religion as a mechanism for the social good; Such a mechanism is considered useless if it is not employed to contribute to a specific change in the world. For a Millennial, it makes no sense to attend a church that does not act on the values they believe to be true. Organized religion must in this case seek to understand the needs of this generation by genuinely striving to build an environment open to debate and adaptation."[9]

The first Forgotten Luther symposium concentrated its efforts on "reclaiming the social-economic dimension of the Reformation," as the title of the book clearly states.[10] It is precisely this Luther and the movement he led that invigorate our young adults to consider a life of service to the neighbor as their vocation. Upon their reentry into US society and congregational life, they still wrestle with the dissonance experienced prior to deployment, which is further heightened during this year of service by the witness of their host congregations and church. Although they do not use this language, they see this work of mercy and justice as the *vocation* of the church. Vocation is much closer to their experience than the notion of mission (with all its historical baggage). As Professor Westhelle reminds us, the Reformation was a "disruptive event." The disruption of alienating and marginalizing structures ("These people who have been turning the world upside down have come here also" [Acts 17:6b]) becomes the dynamo for their vocation. However, rigor mortis sets in quickly: "Grafted in the subconscious of societies affected by it erstwhile, the Reformation hardened into the institutional patterns of European culture and politics. How does an institutional reality become an event again? Or to put it more bluntly, can and should 'Orthodoxy' find its 'heretical' roots again?"[11] Yes, a fossilized reality can become an event again; we just need to let the Spirit rush like a "violent wind" (Acts 2:2).

8. "Cappadocian" refers to the theology articulated by three fourth-century theologians born in Cappadocia (today's Turkey): Basil the Great (330–79), bishop of Caesarea; his brother Gregory (335–95), who became bishop of Nyssa; and their friend Gregory of Nazianzus (320–89) bishop of Constantinople.

9. "The Relationship between Millennials and Spirituality," WeMystic, accessed January 22, 2020, https://tinyurl.com/3w5rw6zj.

10. Carter Lindberg and Paul Wee, eds., *The Forgotten Luther: Reclaiming the Social-Economic Dimension of the Reformation* (Minneapolis: Lutheran University Press, 2016).

11. Westhelle, *Transfiguring Luther*, loc. 226 of 8598.

I regularly remind the YAGM participants and alumni about my ulterior motive for this program: it is an instrument to infiltrate my own (our own) church. This program is showing us how to awaken the "heretic spirit" (Westhelle) of the Reformation. The lessons learned from this program could be helpful in our quest to revitalize our congregational life. The ELCA statistical report shows a steady decline in our membership. Further data from 2018 shows that 67 percent of ELCA congregations baptized three children or less in 2018, and for the first time since the beginning of the ELCA, the number of members who died was higher than the number of people baptized.[12] In many of our congregations, confirmation equals graduation from church. Our youth and young adults are finding the church not being relevant. The YAGM year provides a space for reflection, immersion, and rediscovery. What they find is a church deeply rooted in the "dangerous memory" (Johannes Metz) of Jesus, fully committed to being a sign of the future that is "dancing" (Jürgen Moltmann) into our present.

LUTHER AND MISSION

There has been a long debate on whether the notion of mission was present in the reformers, particularly in Luther. Gustav Warneck posited the view that mission, as he understood it from his nineteenth-century context, was nonexistent in Luther. As I have written elsewhere,[13] this is a matter of definition. If by *mission* we understand the crossing of a border, in this case a geographical one, to share the good news of the gospel, then Luther is guilty as charged. However, I affirm there was a notion of mission seeping through Luther's theological framework. Ingemar Oberg, in his *Luther and World Mission*, challenges Warneck's position, claiming that mission "has been incorrectly defined."[14] Luther saw his "mission field" in his own social location. What he found during the Saxony visitation (1526–28) became the focal point for God's mission among the faithful in Germany.[15] Oberg continues, "Luther does not limit obedience to the

---

12. Evangelical Lutheran Church in America, 2018 Congregational Report, form A.

13. Rafael Malpica Padilla, "Accompaniment as an Alternative Model for the Practice of Mission," *Trinity Seminary Review* 29 (Summer/Fall 2008): 87–96.

14. Ingemar Oberg, *Luther and World Mission: A Historical and Systematic Study with Special Reference to Luther's Bible Exposition*, trans. Dean Apel (St. Louis, MO: Concordia, 2007), 2.

15. As the Evangelical Lutheran Church in America (ELCA) opens itself to a conversation about vitality and innovation, it will be interesting to further study the Saxony visitation as a model for mission. The parallel between the context in Saxony and our times is intriguing. Professor James Scherer captures it beautifully:

Since the gospel had fallen into oblivion in Christendom—Luther's gentiles being those who had never heard the pure word of God preached in Germany—missionary obedience could only mean preaching the gospel anew.

Great Commission to journeys over land and sea. Instead he integrates the work of the church at home and the work of mission abroad. The Reformation itself was mission in the sense that it helped the Gospel find its way to people."[16]

The triad of Jesus, Paul, and Luther has been critical in assisting us in the Global Mission unit of the ELCA to offer an understanding of mission based on a rereading of the creation narrative (which I describe as the "narrative of origins"). This rereading is heavily influenced by the "trinitarian renaissance," particularly the works of Catherine Mowry LaCugna,[17] Leonardo Boff,[18] and Stanley J. Grenz.[19]

Genesis 1:26 gives us a look into our narrative of origins. The much-debated "Let us" points to what God wills for all creation: to be a reflection of God's essence. The extreme relationality that is the essence of God is bestowed on humankind. We were created in relationship and for relationships. As sin entered our human existence, the image of God in us was distorted and fractured. By the end of chapter four, God's mission is to restore community,[20] to remedy the breach wrought by sin to God's plan for creation. Yes, we have come to know the stories in Genesis 3 and 4 as the stories of original sin. However, I deeply believe they speak about the sin against our origins: for we were created in relationship and for relationships!

Of all the New Testament writers, it is Paul (or the Pauline communities) who best captures this notion of God's mission. In the Corinthian correspondence, we read, "So if anyone is in Christ, there is a new creation: everything old has passed away; see, everything has become

---

And since the distortion of the gospel message had led to the degeneration of mission into ecclesiastical propaganda, forced conversion, crusades and nonevangelical methods, Luther's obedience to the mission command meant re-establishing the church on its own true foundation in Jesus Christ and the gospel. For Luther mission was the essential task of the church in every age, but only a church itself grounded in the gospel could do mission.

Quoted by Oberg, *Luther and World Mission*, 9–10.

16. Oberg, 4.

17. Oberg, 4.

18. Leonardo Boff, *Holy Trinity, Perfect Community*, trans. Phillip Berryman (Maryknoll, NY: Orbis, 2000). According to Boff, "In the beginning is the communion of the Three not the solitude of a one." Boff, 1.

19. Stanley J. Grenz, *The Social God and the Relational Self: A Trinitarian Theology of the Imago Dei* (Louisville, KY: Westminster John Knox, 2001).

20. This is the working definition for *mission* in the Global Mission praxis. This definition was the guiding principle as I worked with the Latin American and Caribbean Lutheran churches in developing a strategy for missional engagement. This process led to *accompaniment* as the lens and model for mission. In addition, Professor Craig Nessan, from Wartburg Theological Seminary, building on the Hebrew concept *tikkun olam*, affirms that "God's purpose is to mend the world." See Craig L. Nessan, *Shalom Church: The Body of Christ as a Ministering Community* (Minneapolis: Fortress, 2010), 3. See also Malpica Padilla, "Accompaniment as an Alternative," 87–96.

new! All this is from God, who reconciled us to himself through Christ, and has given us the ministry of reconciliation" (2 Cor 5:17–18). This is God's two-movement symphony of life, and if we want to hear it in a Lutheran key, the *Confessio Augustana* 4 and 6 play it well for us: justification and sanctification. We are freed from our *incurvatus*, the deadly naval gazing that enslaves us. We are freed to serve the neighbor in need. In his "Freedom of a Christian," Luther further expands this call or vocation: "Just as our neighbor is in need and lacks that in which we abound, so we were in need before God and lacked his mercy. Hence, as our heavenly Father has in Christ freely come to our aid, we also ought freely to help our neighbor through our body and its works and each one should become as it were a Christ to the other that we may be Christ to one another and Christ may be the same in all, that is, that we may be truly Christians."[21] Once our chin has been lifted up from looking at our belly button, there is only one thing to do: to engage the other in God's name. And this work—as Luther writes in his sermon on *The Two Kinds of Righteousness*—is our "proper righteousness, not because we alone work it, but because we work with that first and alien righteousness."[22]

If God's mission is to restore community, how does God do it?

SACRAMENTAL ORTHOPRAXIS

In baptism, God creates and sustains the community of the new people of God.[23] We see the other no longer with human eyes but through God's own eyes. Differences cannot be used to exclude people from participation in the community, for all "are one in Christ" (Gal 3:28). Through the baptismal waters, we are claimed by God and given an identity that surpasses the boundaries of geographies or nation-states. I cherish my visits to our companions in India. It is a beautiful country with a rich diversity of cultures and religions, but one in which the sin of casteism is still prevalent. In this worldview, a large segment of the Indian society is denied their personhood. Their mere presence renders others unclean. The overwhelming majority of the members of the Lutheran churches in India come from this marginalized and oppressed sector of society, the

---

21. Martin Luther, "The Freedom of a Christian," 1520, in *LW* 31:367–68.

22. Timothy F. Lull, ed., *Martin Luther's Basic Theological Writings* (Minneapolis: Fortress, 1989), 157.

23. Justo González defines *orthopraxis* as "a term often employed, particularly by liberation theologians to indicate that proper praxis is just as important as proper doctrine—or rather, that a doctrine, no matter how correct, that does not lead to and derive from the praxis of love is flawed." See Justo L. González, *Essential Theological Terms* (Louisville, KY: Westminster John Knox, 2005), 125.

Dalits.[24] Imagine the powerful good news baptism has brought to their lives. Listen with the minds and hearts of Dalit people to a portion of a great baptismal homily recorded in 1 Peter 2:9–10: "But you are a chosen race, a royal priesthood, a holy nation, God's own people, in order that you may proclaim the mighty acts of him who called you out of darkness into his marvelous light. Once you were not a people, but now you are God's people." These powerful words are indeed liberating to the undocumented aliens in Asia Minor—to whom the letter is addressed—to the Dalits in India, and to peoples whose stories and narratives have been suppressed and replaced with stories that allow for their continued exclusion and marginalization. In baptism, God deconstructs these narratives and creates a community that is a reflection of the being of God.

At the table, in the Eucharist, God creates and sustains the community of the equals. It does not matter what you bring—everybody is fed and receives the same gift: "The Holy Supper both feeds us with the body and blood of Christ and awakens our care for the hungry ones of the earth."[25] Around the Table, the egalitarian community of the Three takes place in our midst grafting us into a "perichoretic dance"[26] (Moltmann) with one another celebrating our diversity as God's gift to humankind.

In our tradition, we have been concerned that the sacraments have been "rightly administered,"[27] but I contend that our major challenge is for the sacraments to be rightly understood. Baptism and the Eucharist are powerful symbols that point to the ultimate reality, the eschatological community of God's sovereign rule. Although this community is the making of God alone, I believe that here and now, in an imperfect and transitory manner, we live in that kind of community. Geerhardus J. Vos, professor at Princeton in the early twentieth century, coined the famous phrase "Already but not yet." Luther and his understanding of baptism and the Eucharist assist us to live in the "not yet," in this liminal space as we move forward to the future of God. The sacraments have a powerful and radical meaning, but we have domesticated them to fit the cultic and ritual lives of our ecclesial communities. The sacraments continue to be hostages of an individualized religious experience that strips them of their

24. Dalits are members of the lowest cast in India and commonly known as "untouchables." Although the Indian constitution abolished untouchability, in practice, certain "polluting" tasks continue to be assigned to the scheduled castes.

25. *The Use of the Means of Grace: A Statement on the Practice of Word and Sacrament* (Chicago: ELCA, 1997), 56.

26. The Greek term *perichoresis* means mutual indwelling. For Moltmann, each of the personas in the Trinity lives in one another. This mutual indwelling is the basis for the oneness in the Godhead. This movement of mutual indwelling, sustained and created by love, is what he describes as the dance of love.

27. "Augsburg Confession," in *The Book of Concord: The Confessions of the Evangelical Lutheran Church*, trans. and ed. Theodore G. Tappert (Philadelphia: Fortress, 1959), sec. 7, 32.

radical and transformational nature. Professor Craig Nessan has warned us about this disease: "The church in the North American context faces the disease of a rampant individualism that conceives religiosity primarily as a matter of personal preferences rather than communal responsibility."[28]

Baptism incorporates us into the body of Christ (1 Cor 12:27), and this body (*soma Christou*) should not be construed as a closed community. To be "in Christ," and of Christ, means being open to the ways, radical and new ways, in which God continues to incorporate people into the body of Christ. In such a fragmented society as ours—torn apart by issues of race, place of origin, sexual and gender identities, sexism, and many other "isms"—we proclaim that there is a place for you in this community. In baptism, God has claimed us, all of us, creating a community free of boundaries, whose identity is found not in its homogeneity but given through our participation in the life, death, and resurrection of Jesus, the Christ. We are an open and inclusive community of followers of Jesus serving others in need.

The issue of boundaries is also present at the table. This is one of the problems Paul addressed in Corinth. Some of the members, because of their position in society, were able to come to the meal before others—the laborers—had the opportunity to sit in. This problem is not atypical of the society in which norms for communal meals originated. There was a certain "banquet ideology,"[29] which communicated social values, established social boundaries that determined who could participate, how to sit, and so on. This ideology is behind the meal controversy at Corinth, and Paul challenges this behavior by pointing to the "social equity and social obligation"[30] of the Lord's Supper. Luther expands this notion of the "social responsibility" of the Eucharist in his treatise on *The Blessed Sacrament of the Holy and True Body of Christ, and the Brotherhoods*. Listen to Luther:

> Here your heart must go out in life and learn that this is a sacrament of love. As love and support are given you, you in turn must render love and support to Christ in his needy ones.[31]

> For the sacrament has no blessing and significance unless love grows daily and so changes a person that he is made one with all others.[32]

---

28. Nessan, *Shalom Church*, 1.

29. Dennis E. Smith, *From Symposium to Eucharist: The Banquet in the Early Christian World* (Minneapolis: Fortress, 2003).

30. Smith, 175.

31. Lull, *Luther's Basic Theological Writings*, 188.

32. Lull, 190.

Thus by means of this sacrament all self-seeking love is rooted out and gives place to that which seeks the common good of all.[33]

During the regime of Ferdinand Marcos, Father Edmond Delatorio served as a priest in the Philippines. He was imprisoned for advocating in favor of the oppressed and the poor. He asked a guard for bread and wine to celebrate the daily Eucharist. His cell mate joined in the celebration, and soon thereafter, the whole cell block was participating in this liturgy of life. When the news reached the warden, he immediately issued an order: "No more bread and wine to Father Delatorio because bread and wine in the hands of this priest become a revolutionary weapon."

The right practice of our sacramental identity is liberating and trans-formative. As people who claim this theological identity (Lutheran), we must ask ourselves, What are the sociological implications of our theo-logical affirmations? When was the last time that we saw our pastors, or ourselves, as revolutionaries as we celebrated God's presence in our midst—amid this broken world—through water, wine, and bread?

So what's next? Professor Westhelle gives us a clue: "The theology of the cross is neither a discourse nor a doctrine. It is a way of life that we live out. It is a practice that involves a risk. It is a story that if truly told, courts danger but moves also into hopeful solidarity, the solidarity of those who are moved by the pain of God in the midst of the world, or by the pain of the world in the midst of God."[34]

THE THIRD SACRAMENT

There has been extensive conversation, and speculation, about a pos-sible third sacrament among Lutherans. Both Luther and the *Apology of the Augsburg Confession* refer to absolution as that possible third sacrament. My reading of Luther from my Latinx context and the praxis of mission through the Global Mission unit programs leads me in another direction (and I say this with a little bit of fear and trembling, for I am not a Luther scholar). The Smalcald Articles is Luther's theological testament,[35] and

---

33. Lull, 195.

34. Vítor Westhelle, *The Scandalous God: The Use and Abuse of the Cross* (Minneapolis: Fortress, 2006), ix–x. See also the work of Japanese Lutheran theologian Kazoh Kitamori, *The Theology of the Pain of God* (Eugene, OR: Wipf & Stock, 2006).

35. "I wanted to do this so that those who live and remain after me will have my testimony and confession to presser, in addition to the confession that I have already published." Quoted in Robert Kolb and Timothy Wengert, eds., *The Book of Concord* (Minneapolis: Fortress, 2000), 298.

in article 4, Luther talks about how the gospel "gives guidance and help against sin."[36] In addition to the word and the sacraments, Luther mentions "the mutual conversation and consolation of brothers and sisters."[37] This is the third sacrament, when people freed by the gospel and bound to one another live together the "already but not yet," not as a refuge from the world, but as the place from which we are sent into the "pain of the world." Yes, when Luther used this phrase, he had in mind the monastic practice of mutual confession, but in my reappropriation of Luther, I see and use this notion to describe something beyond the mutuality of two individuals. As God, through the Spirit, brings people together in Jesus Christ, this gathered community becomes his (Jesus's) body and an instrument for God to achieve God's purposes for the world. We Lutherans are not used to speaking of the church as a "sacrament" to the world; however, it is a vigorous instrument to call people into the fellowship of God, a fellowship that transcends all barriers that exclude and separate us from one another. This notion of a vibrant church deeply rooted in our broken reality is what captivates our YAGM participants and hopefully is turning them into the "new heretics" so badly needed in our faith communities and the institutional church known as the ELCA.

The 1995 ELCA social statement on peace (*For Peace in God's World*) puts forth a very healthy understanding of the church as she "fulfills the mandates of its divine calling."[38] As such, the church becomes a serving and reconciling presence in the world. These are descriptors that most ELCA members will wholeheartedly endorse or appropriate. But the statement does not end there. It continues to affirm that the church, as it fulfills her calling, is also a disturbing presence in the world "when it refuses to be silent and instead speaks the truth" when people only want to hear everything is fine and confine her to its religious space. Almost thirty years ago, at the Luther Colloquia sponsored by the Institute for Luther Studies at Gettysburg Seminary, I heard Professor Eric Gritsch state that for Luther, "Christ starts all insurrections by confronting the world with the Gospel." He was paraphrasing Luther's statement in "A Sincere Admonition by Martin Luther to All Christians to Guard against Insurrection and Rebellion," where Luther says that "Christ himself has already begun an insurrection with his mouth."[39] The word that frees us, binds us to one another, and sends the church of Jesus Christ to participate in his mission is that "revolutionary weapon" that Bishop Medardo Gomez used in El Salvador, Bishop Manas Buthelezi in South Africa, and Bishop

---

36. Kolb and Wengert, 319.
37. Kolb and Wengert, 319.
38. *For Peace in God's World* (Chicago: ELCA, 1995), 4.
39. "A Sincere Admonition by Martin Luther to All Christians to Guard against Insurrection and Rebellion," 1522, in *LW* 45:67–68.

Zephania Kameeta in Namibia. Christ indeed has begun an insurrection with his mouth!

> To be your presence is our mission bold,
> To feed the poor and shelter homeless cold,
> To be your hands of justice, right uphold, Alleluia!
>
> To be your presence is our mission blest,
> To speak for all broken and oppressed,
> To be your voice of hope, your love expressed, Alleluia!
>
> We are your heart, O Christ, your hands and voice,
> To serve your people is our call and choice,
> And in this mission we, the church, rejoice, Alleluia![40]

STUDY QUESTIONS

1. How does the YAGM program help reawaken the spirit of the Reformation? What other programs or ministries in the church have helped change or shape your understanding of the church's role in the world?
2. What does it mean to be "created in relationship and for relationships"?
3. What does it mean to be part of the community created in baptism and Holy Communion?
4. What does it mean to you to be the church in the world today? Where is God calling the church to be?

---

40. ELCA, "To Be Your Presence," in *Evangelical Lutheran Worship* (Minneapolis: Augsburg Fortress, 2006), hymn 546.

Contributors

Rev. Dr. Karen L. Bloomquist is a theologian-at-large who has been a parish pastor (in California, New York City, and Washington) and a seminary professor and administrator (Lutheran School of Theology at Chicago, Wartburg Seminary, and Pacific Lutheran Seminary), directed the department through which the Evangelical Lutheran Church in America (ELCA) developed its first social statements, and was director of the Department for Theology and Studies of the Lutheran World Federation (LWF; Geneva). She has edited and written many articles and books, including *The Dream Betrayed: Religious Challenge of the Working Class* (1990) and *Seeing-Remembering-Connecting: Subversive Practices of Being Church* (2016). In early 2019, she taught at the United Theological College in Bangalore, India.

Rev. Conrad A. Braaten, an ELCA parish pastor for over four decades, is responsible for initiating the Forgotten Luther project. A graduate of St. Olaf College and Luther Seminary (St. Paul, Minnesota), he worked in parish ministry and with social ministries in Florida, where he was also involved with the Florida-Bahamas Synod's companion church in the Caribbean and South America. While serving on the Board of World Mission of the American Lutheran Church (ALC), he was active with program initiatives in Central America and for a decade was a member of the USA Steering Committee of the LWF's Caribbean-Haiti Program. Prior to retiring in 2012 as senior pastor of Lutheran Church of the Reformation in Washington, DC, Braaten was on the churchwide staff of the ELCA's Division for Congregational Life in the program areas of urban ministry and congregational social ministry. He has developed and resourced congregational leadership programs and coordinated and led more than two dozen educational immersions to countries in the Caribbean, Central America, and South America. Now retired to Arizona with his wife, Jennifer, a retired college president, he continues to work with the church in areas of advocacy and global mission.

Dr. Ryan P. Cumming, is the program director for hunger education with ELCA World Hunger. In this role, he directs the development of ELCA World Hunger's educational resources, researches trends in hunger and poverty, and supports communications with partners and congregations. As an educator and researcher, he has presented his work on theology, ethics, and religious experiences to scholarly and ecclesial audiences and has served as a consultant and presenter on pedagogy, active learning, and instructional design. He also teaches undergraduate courses on theological ethics and religious studies at Central Michigan University and Loyola University Chicago. Cumming is the author of *The African American Challenge to Just War Theory* (Palgrave, 2013) and contributor to and coeditor of the three-volume *Forgotten Luther* series, published by Lutheran University Press and Fortress Press. He is a former interim editor of the *Journal of Lutheran Ethics* and was a member of the ELCA's criminal justice social statement task force.

Dr. Guillermo Hansen is professor of global Christianity, societies, and cultures and Martin Luther King Chair for Justice and Christian Community at Luther Theological Seminary, St. Paul, Minnesota. A native of Argentina, Hansen served as director of postgraduate and doctoral studies at Ecumenical Theological University in Buenos Aires (2003–8) and vice president of the United Evangelical Lutheran Church of Argentina and Uruguay. Hansen received the master of divinity degree from Ecumenical Theological University in Buenos Aires (1986); the master of sacred theology degree from Trinity Lutheran Seminary, Columbus, Ohio (1988); and the master of theology degree (1990) and the doctor of philosophy degree (1995) from the Lutheran School of Theology at Chicago (LSTC). He also served as a theological advisor to the Department of Theological Studies in the LWF (1997–2003). Among his many articles are "¿Casus Confessionus? La Globalización Neoliberal y Nuestra Confesión de Fe," in *Para que puedan resistir: Las Iglesias luteranas latinoamericanas frente a la globalización neoliberal y la deuda externa*, ed. R. Krüger, 141–64 (Buenos Aires: LWF and Ecumenical Theological University, 2004); and "Neoliberal Globalization: A Casus Confessionis?," in *Communion, Responsibility, Accountability: Responding as a Lutheran Communion to Neoliberal Globalization*, ed. Karen Bloomquist, 163–78 (Geneva: LWF, 2004).

Dr. Carter Lindberg is professor emeritus of church history at the Boston University School of Theology. Previous academic positions include the following: research professor at the LWF's Institute of Ecumenical Research, Strasbourg, France (1979–82); the College of the Holy Cross, Worcester, Massachusetts (1967–72); and Susquehanna University,

Selinsgrove, Pennsylvania (1965–67). He graduated from Augustana College (Illinois), Lutheran School of Theology at Chicago, and the University of Iowa School of Religion. He has contributed a wealth of research to the field of Reformation studies including *Beyond Charity: Reformation Initiatives for the Poor* (Fortress, 1993) and *The European Reformations* (Wiley-Blackwell, 2010). His recent publications include the following: coeditor (with Paul Wee) and contributor, *The Forgotten Luther: Reclaiming the Social-Economic Dimension of the Reformation* (Minneapolis: Lutheran University Press, 2016); "Luther on a Market Economy," *Lutheran Quarterly* 30 (2016): 373–92; and also *The European Reformations* (2nd ed., 2010), *Love: A Brief History* (2008), *A Brief History of Christianity* (2005), and *The Pietist Theologians* (2004), all with Wiley-Blackwell.

Rev. Rafael Malpica Padilla serves as the executive director for the Global Mission unit of the ELCA. He has been with the Global Mission unit since 1993. Prior to his ministry at the ELCA's churchwide office, he served as bishop of the Caribbean synod as the ELCA came together in 1988. One of Malpica Padilla's contributions to the world of mission is his articulation of *accompaniment* as the methodological tool and hermeneutical key for the praxis of mission. He holds a master of divinity degree from the Lutheran Theological Seminary at Philadelphia (1981) and several honorary degrees from institutions in the United States and India.

Rev. Dr. Ishmael Noko is the founder and president of the Interfaith Action for Peace in Africa, a pan-African program initiated in 2002 during Africa's first continent-wide interfaith summit meeting; an ordained pastor of the Evangelical Lutheran Church of Zimbabwe; and the current CEO and principal of Luther Varsity in Southern Africa, a private higher education institution. Noko previously served as head of the Department of Theology / Religious Studies and dean of the Faculty of Humanities at the University of Botswana. In 1994, he was elected as the first African general secretary of the LWF. Noko earned two graduate degrees in Canada: a master's degree at the Lutheran Theological Seminary in Saskatoon and a PhD from McGill University in Quebec.

Rev. Dr. Mitri Raheb is the founder and president of Dar al-Kalima University College of Arts and Culture in Bethlehem. The most widely published Palestinian theologian to date, Raheb is the author and editor of nineteen books. He served as the senior pastor of Christmas Lutheran Church in Bethlehem from 1987 to 2017 and as the president of the Synod of the Evangelical Lutheran Church in Jordan and the Holy Land from 2011 to 2016. He is a member of the Palestinian National Council and the Palestinian Central Council and serves as an advisor to the Higher

Presidential Palestinian Committee on Church Affairs. A social entrepreneur, Raheb has founded several Institutions and is the cofounder of Bright Stars of Bethlehem, a multifaceted program of education in Palestine. In 2017, he received the Tolerance Award, in 2015 the Olof Palme Prize, in 2012 the German Media Prize, and in 2007 the well-known German Peace Award of Aachen. Raheb's work has received wide media attention, including from CNN, ABC, CBS, *60 Minutes*, BBC, ARD, ZDF, DW, BR, *NZZ*, Raiuno, Stern, *Economist, Newsweek, Herald Tribune,* Al-Jazeera, Al-Mayadin, and *Vanity Fair.*

Rev. Dr. Paul A. Wee retired from his position as adjunct professor at the Elliott School of International Affairs, George Washington University, Washington, DC. Wee and his wife, Rene, now reside in Lacey, Washington, closer to their three children and two grandchildren. Following his work as international theological director of the Luther Center in Wittenberg, Germany, he served as program officer in the Religion and Peacemaking unit of the United States Institute of Peace (USIP), working primarily on interfaith conflict resolution in Nigeria and Colombia. He received his BA, cum laude, from Harvard University; a master of divinity degree from Luther Seminary; and a PhD, magna cum laude, in philosophy and social science from the University of Berlin. He worked in eastern and central Europe, primarily with faith-based communities, during the communist period and was awarded the Order of Merit (first class) from the Federal Republic of Germany for his work. He was a member of the Faculty of Theology of the University of Oxford and served as general secretary of Lutheran World Ministries and assistant general secretary for International Affairs and Human Rights of the Geneva-based LWF.